Give Only Love

TAG Publishing, LLC
2030 S. Milam
Amarillo, TX 79109
www.TAGPublishers.com
Office (806) 373-0114
Fax (806) 373-4004
info@TAGPublishers.com

ISBN: 978-1-59930-411-3

First Edition

Give Only Love

Joseph Nealon

Contents

Dedication

I dedicate this book to my children, Samantha and Kyle. We are with each other for a reason. We may not know exactly what that reason is or why we do what we do, but I know this to be true: no matter what you do in life, what you say or how you feel about me, I will always love both of you unconditionally.

My second dedication is to myself, thank you for this opportunity to allow me to grow and simply be who I am.

Acknowledgements

I would first, and foremost, like to thank my parents.

To my mother, who gave me the gift of laughter.

To my father, who made me understand this is the greatest gift of all. I love you both unconditionally. I could not have chosen better parents.

To Bob Proctor, who was the first person that taught me about the power that lies within all of us 28 years ago with his wonderful book, *You Were Born Rich* and his seminars.

To Sandy French who, through his love of books and thirst for knowledge, inspired me to fall in love with both books and with the quest for the meaning of life.

To my brother Mike, I know you are on the right path because of the love that lies within every action that you do and every thought that you think. I could not have asked for a better brother; you humble me. Every time I see you, I see the divinity that lies within us all.

To my sister, Patti, whose help with my business can never be measured. You are an angel and I love you dearly.

To my sister, Brenda: time, distance and choices that we make in life only separate us if we allow them to. We may not always agree with each other's choices, but that does not mean I don't love you.

To Dr. Hew Len, who's teaching of love helped me like no other to understand what it is to love and the power it holds.

To my in-laws, I owe a debt of gratitude for helping me to go on a journey of a life time. Thank you.

To Caroline, being together for over a quarter of a century, we shared a lot of memories that I will always treasure. May you know only peace and experience only love.

To my children, Samantha and Kyle, you are my greatest teachers. The lessons that I have learned and am learning are priceless. I know you are both hurt and angry with me right now and that's ok. Life is not about feeling angry, hurt, lost or scared, but about the lessons that these experiences teach us. We each chose this life - find out why. I love you with all my heart and always will unconditionally.

Introduction

"If you understood my objective for writing this book you would Love my Life"
Thanks Ian

In life, you believe one of four things:

1. That you are born, die and that's it.
2. That you are born, die, and then go to heaven or hell.
3. That you are born, die, then reincarnate repeatedly - therefore it does not matter what we do in this life.
4. That you are born, die, reincarnate repeatedly and it does matter what you do in this life.

This book deals with the fourth option: that we live forever and it does matter what we do while we are here.

This book is my life-long quest for the answer to two questions:

1. What is life all about?
2. Why am I here?

These are two questions that I think we all should ask and that this book ventures to answer.

I have spent 28 years studying countless authors and hundreds of books on the topic of life's purpose. Some books I have read more than 30 times. I have also viewed countless videos, attended a multitude of seminars and debates and engaged in extensive self-analysis to come up with the answer to these two important questions.

I know these two questions will lead to more questions, but in my mind, these are the two that need to be asked first and foremost.

One of the dedications of this book is to myself and, if you truly grasp what I am about to say, you will get a little insight as to what this book is really about. I can only write these words and concepts for myself; I am the only person I can actually change. The rest of you are on your own journey and are mere players upon my stage of life, as I am on yours

You are here to help me with my lessons as I am here to help you with yours.

My intention is not for you to read this book and follow me. I want you to read this book and learn to follow yourself – the real you. I want you to be the best you can be and learn to trust the voice that is within all of us.

If you're a Catholic lawyer who has five kids – great. If you are a Muslim doctor with no children - perfect. If you are a painter, bus driver, farmer or factory worker, it does not matter. Just learn to follow your inner joy no matter where that takes you or what the world tells you.

I am writing this book like I started my business – just because I think I can. I have never written a book before, got C's in English and, quite honestly, am not that smart.

It has nothing to do with any of that and everything to do with the voice within telling me to write this book. So, I just listen and believe I will be guided to where I need to be, when I need to be there.

You may assume that I write this from the pedestal of a perfect life. Well, here is another bomb. I am a going through a divorce, yet I am writing about LOVE. How is that even possible? How can a guy who has lived a less than pristine life write a book about LOVE?

I can because I think that I can. Whatever each one of us believes we can do, we can. We are all worthy. Repeat after me:

We are all worthy. Burn that into your mind until you believe it. There has never been a person that has ever lived, or will ever live, that is not worthy.

Within these pages, you are going to learn that unconditional love and forgiveness are essential to happiness. Yet, to reach those higher concepts, you must start with yourself. You are going to learn that it is okay to be you.

There is a quote I love that is attributed to Oscar Wilde. It states, "You must be yourself – everyone else is taken!"

And this is true. You must learn to be comfortable in your own skin with who you are deep down.

You will also learn that you are 100% responsible 100% of the time for everything that goes on in your life, so be careful what you focus your thoughts on. When you have faith in what you are doing and you get emotionally attached to your goal, you can combine those with supreme effort and unconditional love - at which point ANYTHING IS POSSIBLE.

I had a high school geography teacher that once told me that I should do everyone a favor and quit – quit trying, quit school, quit life. He told me that I was taking up space and would never amount to anything.

I just want to take this time to thank him for forcing me to see my own lack of commitment to who I could become and say to him that I am sorry for causing so much annoyance in his life.

While it may have sounded cruel at the time, that one comment has helped me immensely over the years. It still does today, as it spurs me on to be the best I can be each day.

All my life, I felt as though everyone I came into contact with was telling me to wake up. Wake up - wake up to what? I know now it is to wake up to the self within myself, to wake up and be who I was meant to be.

Deciding to write this book was no small thing and, though my conscious mind protested greatly, I did it anyway. Now, I no longer feel that people are telling me to wake up. I am at peace with who I am.

When a person read books like this about the essence of life, spirituality or some metaphysical connection to the larger universe, they get the impression that the person writing the book now has a perfect life and every moment is filled with joy and happiness.

Let me assure you that it is not that the circumstances you encounter each day change, but, rather, that you learn to control your state of being as it relates to those same circumstances.

In other words, though you may shovel the same crap every day, you perceive it differently and learn to use it to your benefit.

Finally, you will realize that you constantly change the future and the past by how you perceive it right now; you are simply more diligent about how you respond to life's events today. Some friends of mine, who know that I am writing a book, guess that it will be filled with information and antidotes about how I was successful or grew my business.

So, for those people here is a summary of things that helped me own my own business:

1. I just simply thought I could.

2. I visualized myself making $2 Million per year and got emotionally attached to how that made me feel.

3. Whenever there is a big decision to make regarding my business, I do what the owner of Sony did and swallow the opportunity (notice I didn't say problem, because there are no problems - just opportunities). If it gives me indigestion, I don't do it.

4. Henry Ford was asked which was more important: sales, production or finance? He answered by asking what was the most important leg on a 3-legged stool. He meant that they are all important and interdependent. Ford also said that he may not be able to build, sell or finance a car but he could hire someone that could. I approach my business the same way.

5. My friends who taught me to ski said that if you are not falling down, you are not pushing hard enough to see how great you can be.

6. All great people will face some adversity that, at the time, seems insurmountable. Therefore, welcome adverse conditions for what they are - opportunities to be great.

7. Everyone else comes first: customers, suppliers and employees.

8. When I didn't think we were going to make, it I remembered what my geography teacher said: that I was a waste of space and would never amount to anything.

There it is, the shortest business book on record! This is not a business book, though many of the principles certainly could apply to business.

But life isn't about business; it is about humanity and who you really are - not what you do.

It is not what you do in life that matters, but how you do what you do.

Life is a journey, an adventure that allows you to experience what you need to experience for the progression of your soul. This book is simply a story of my journey, the experiences I had along the way and how it made me grow and change into who I am.

If you gain even a glimmer of truth you can apply to your life, then it has certainly been worth it. Yet, know that I wrote these words as part of my own journey, my own growth - not to be some guru telling you how to live. Only you can do that.

Since my journey will never end, I can assume that the experiences I will have will never end either. They will grow and build on one another into infinity.

May your own journey teach you the lessons that you were meant to learn - whatever they may be. I use the term 'learning' because most of us have forgotten who we are; you need only remember who you actually are - then all things will be known to you.

The following is part of a song I wrote 17 years ago in Santa Fe:

"When I tell myself 'tomorrow'…

What I really mean is 'goodbye'…

Because tomorrow never comes…

And dreams just simply die."

I wrote this book so my dream would not just simply die. I hope that someday it will help someone. I soon realized, however, that it already has help someone - me. I have no expectations for this book other than the experience of writing it. May it find its way to the people who it is suppose to find - nothing more, nothing less. We acquire knowledge in order to gain wisdom. This helps us live the lives that we came here to live.

Chapter 1

Sleeping with the Lights on

Think about all the times that you've slept with the lights on in your life. Maybe there was a night that a thunderstorm scared the bejesus out of you when you were nine; maybe there was a night, as a pre-teen, when you saw "Psycho" for the first time.

But how many times as a grown adult have you ever slept with the lights on? Not many, I'd guess, and this is certainly true for me too. I never slept with the lights on; I mean, why would I? What on earth did I have to fear, right?

It may sound kind of ridiculous, but I'll admit that it happened to me one night. I had an experience so powerful that I lay in bed all alone at a little hotel in northern Ontario called "The Moose Motel" (yes that's its real name), with eyes wide open and the lights on the whole night.

It was one of those experiences that makes your nerves stand on end for hours and the adrenaline rush through your blood so fast it whooshes through your head like a raging river. I'll tell you right now that, even though I was a grown man of 35 years old, no amount of money could have made me turn the lights off that night and morning couldn't have come fast enough.

That night was the first real step to my discovering that there is more to life than work.

In fact, there is far more beyond what I ever thought possible. Now, understand that there had been several times in my life that I thought there was more to life then what I was experiencing and I'm sure other people feel the same on occasion. I hadn't given a great deal of thought to the spiritual side of life, nor had I contemplated the 'big' questions of life like "why are we here?" or "what my life might mean in the grand scheme of the universe?" I figured there was some guy sitting in an ashram on a mountain somewhere in Tibet worrying about that stuff, so I just didn't.

My partners and I started a business when I was around 30 and it was growing, but I wanted more and, of course, I thought 'more' meant more money. I believed in the whole idea that more money makes you happier ; who doesn't believe that when they are young? Our company distributed food ingredients and chemicals to the food and confectionary industry. My part of the business was the sales side and I wanted to make sure that I held up my end of things. Now, don't get me wrong; I'm not the most serious guy in the world. In fact, some people would say that I joke too much. I have been known to make a big mess of things on occasion – been there, done that.

I started looking for ways to improve my performance and, thus, the company's performance. When I was in my mid-twenties, I was just starting out. That was when college graduates made about $40,000 or so. But, I was making $11,500. My wife was making $18,000. We were scraping by, but just barely. I really wanted to figure out how to make more money, so I went to some seminars that were being held close by and the speaker was Bob Proctor, who taught about how to bring more wealth into all areas of your life. It was the very first time I'd ever encountered the idea that thoughts are things. He explained that what we think creates our reality and if we worry about money or try to force our way to wealth, it just doesn't work. At this time, I was studying at least 2 hours a day reading all kinds of self-help books and educational materials to get a better understanding of all the different concepts that were out there.

It was a revolutionary idea to me that you could 'think' yourself to wealth, but also one that made a lot of sense. So, my wife and I were making $29,500 and I visualized us making $65,000 a year combined with a house that was paid for.

I also visualized having good health and being happy, but I saw monetary results very quickly.

Just a few months after I started this visualization, we wanted to buy a home.

I knew from the seminars that one of the things in this process is that you have to leap in.

You have to have faith - and I did. In fact, the real secret is to see yourself with the money and imagine how it feels to own your own home just as if it's happened already - in the present. Get emotionally attached to the thoughts and feelings of ownership (this is a key idea). Then, give this off to the universe and let it go because your only responsibility is to hold the picture; the universe will do the rest. I bought a townhouse for $90,000 (even though I had no money) in the fall of 1985, just after I started meditating that I had a fully paid off home. To make it happen, I had to come up with $5,000 deposit, but I had no clue where the money would come from.

I didn't realize at the time that my dad had already planned to give me a gift of $7,500 when we got married. He had given that to my two sisters when they got married, but I didn't know that. The $7,500 covered my deposit, but then we got word we had to come up with another $3000. It didn't faze me because I'd already seen results with my visualization and we were fully committed to the idea it would happen - which is another secret to manifesting what you want. Understandably, my wife was another story. She worried and said things like, "Oh my God! How are we going to do it? We don't have the money! We can't come up with the money!" In the midst of building this townhouse (construction took longer than expected), I received an extra bonus that was just enough to cover what we needed.

Meanwhile, as we waited for our townhouse to be built, I kept visualizing that our salaries would increase to $65,000. To my amazement, within 90 days, we pushed through that mark and beyond! So, I raised my visualized goal higher.

We lived in an apartment while the townhouse was under construction and it took months!

The interesting thing is that all this happened in the 1980's, during what was one of the biggest housing price booms that Canada has ever experienced. We bought the home for $90,000, but the day we moved in it had almost doubled in price.

After about six months, we decided to cash out and we sold our town home in 48 hours for $209,000! We took the profit, added some to it and paid $154,000 in cash for our first home.

This really sent a huge message to me, at age 25, that boy - this really works! Of course, if you're a skeptic, you might say that I just got lucky. But, I know better. I went from having no money and just squeaking by to owning a home outright and having an income that had more than doubled.

As the years ticked by, I was 28 and then 29. I grew tired of working hard for someone else to end up with all the profit. I decided that if I could bring one or two ideas into being, then why couldn't I create my own business? My company, Nealanders, was born out of that idea and proved to me, once again, that thoughts are things and the mind has tremendous power.

I worked very hard on the sales side of the business and I'd already had the experience of trying to force what I wanted in sales situations, which was a disaster. I realized that the negative thoughts and fears that I carried around brought about my frustrations in the company's sales growth. Not that I'm a negative person at all; in fact, I can be super positive and I like being that way. But, we all have fears and insecurities that can creep in and it blocks our progress. That fear is the greatest thief of our happiness.

So, I took these ideas of visualizing what I wanted and decided to start implementing them in the business.

I focused on what I wanted - not the sales levels where they were, but where we wanted them to be.

At the time, our company's sales were sitting at about $6 Million annually, but they weren't growing like I knew they could. So, I wrote down my goals and created notes that said we were a $20 Million dollar company and put them throughout the office. I put them in desk drawers and behind doors. Everywhere any person might look, they would see that number and be reminded of where we were going. Now I had a couple of partners – one of whom was not exactly a paragon of positivity.

He said, "That is completely ridiculous, you need to get a grip on reality!" He got more and more frustrated with me when he kept finding these notes that stated we were a $20 Million dollar company. Finally, one day he said, "Enough already! I get it! We are a $20 Millioncompany! Are you happy now?"

Grinning from ear to ear, I said, "Yes!" It was going to be a lot easier to accomplish this goal with everyone believing. Belief is essential. You can say what you want as a goal but if you really don't believe, you end up blocking that good from coming to you.

Of course, I didn't share all that I'd learned or what I was up to. We were a very business focused partnership and for me to show up in my Moses robes and proclaim (in my best Charlton Hesston voice of course!) that I'd had an epiphany of positivity would not have gone over very well. So, I just ignored the comments and kept right on focusing on what I could do and how I could attract more sales. And it worked! Our company's sales steadily increased - and at an increasing rate.

By the time I was 35 I was working a lot. When I say a lot, I mean 60-hour weeks. They were hard hours, the kind where you are going and going and can't hardly even break for lunch. The business was doing well, but it was still in the building stage, so it needed all of our focused attention all the time. I'll be the first to admit that I was getting burned out.

Things were happening fast and going well as far as sales, which I wanted, but most of the time, it seemed like from the second I showed up in the morning I was going full speed just trying to keep all the balls in the air. I was often exhausted, frustrated and had this anger I couldn't exactly explain. I had put out there that I wanted wealth and wanted to grow the company, but even though it was happening, it was draining me.

At the time, I had a young family (a wife and a baby daughter). My wife's family lived in far northern Ontario, so several times during the year they would come down and stay for a week or so. That eventually got stretched to the point to where one or both would stay six or seven weeks per year. I was very lucky my in-laws are good people, but we didn't always see eye to eye on everything and, as often happens when you stay under the same roof for a while, things can bubble to the surface. They lived a good distance away and we welcomed them. During this time when I was feeling exhausted and drained, they were staying with us for one of these extended visits.

I was coming home late a lot of times and was mentally and physically exhausted. Sometimes when I got home, there were people over that I really didn't know.

My mother-in law (lovingly) would often take over the kitchen and invite people over unbeknownst to us. It wasn't that big of a deal, but in my mind, I made it into a bigger deal than it was. It just got on my nerves not knowing when it might happen and I'll admit my patience was running thin already.

Of course, being of Irish German heritage, the word patience was almost a foreign word to me to begin with! There were also times that my in-laws would go out and not let us know whether to expect them for dinner or not. Again, not a big deal, but the annoyance kind of stacked up and created tension between me and my wife, and me and them.

So, one night I decided to have a chat with my in laws and clear the air. I'm sure you can already see that this plan was flawed from the start, but I didn't see it and assumed all would go well.

It was a Friday night and my wife had gone to bed. I was with my in-laws down in the basement. We were having a good talk, so I thought it was a perfect chance to calmly set out my three requests for them. They were simple: first, let us cook in our own kitchen; second, let us know when guests would be over; third, let us know if we need to expect them for dinner. It seemed really easy and straightforward to me. My requests were very reasonable from my perspective, so of course I knew they would understand. We enjoyed having them there; we just needed to get on the same page about these few items and all would be well, right? Wrong. Micheline, my wife's mother, stormed out and refused to speak to me. She was furious.

I sat there stunned. Dick, my father in law, didn't know what to say. He just shook his head and said, "Well now you've pissed her off. Way to go." What? Why was I the jerk? I was being made to feel bad for having a conversation with them? It would have been different if I thought I was wrong, but I knew I was just trying to make the situation better for everyone.

Anger filled me from head to toe – the kind of anger when you are close to the edge and you know it. I went to the kitchen and grabbed a couple of beers from the refrigerator and took a walk. I fumed as I stomped off down the gravel road. How could these people be so ungrateful? I just had a few simple requests! Are you kidding me?

I played it over in my mind as I felt the rage of seemingly justifiable anger grow. I finally finished one beer and chunked it into the darkness. It hit a big tree – that's when it dawned on me that I was a ways out in the woods. Now realize, we live out in the countryside in southwest Ontario.

It's not the Amazon, but you would not want to run into a pack of wolves or coyotes – and it's dark, very dark. It was exactly the kind of situation that gives you a little chill up your spine.

I looked around for a minute, but then I thought, "I don't care if there is wolf, coyote or whatever out there. If they are looking for an easy target they have picked the wrong guy tonight!" I was so angry, I felt like I could have torn up anything nature had to throw at me. That's probably why the woods were unusually quiet that night – even nature knows when to back off!

I finally made my way back to the house and, a few hours later, calmed down somewhat. By then, it was about two in the morning, so I went to bed thinking that everyone was probably cooling off and by morning it would work itself out. I had planned to go golfing with my dad the next day, so I got up very early, picked up my dad and we went golfing as planned.

Later that day, I walked into the house and found devastated chaos. It was as if all hell had broken loose.

My wife, Caroline, was crying inconsolably. The in-laws were gone. Apparently Mich and Dick had spent the morning berating my wife about how I was the devil and how they would never be back to our house. Then they called my wife's brother, Ricky, to pick them up. It was a nightmare and I was even angrier than I had been the night before, which I didn't know was even possible until right at that moment.

How could parents treat their daughter this way? My wife cried for hours. I called Ricky and he agreed to bring Mich and Dick back over to see if we could talk. They came back, but nothing had changed and the conversation disintegrated pretty quickly. At one point, I ended up toe to toe with Dick, who was an ex NHL athlete and not a little guy! I was sick of their emotional drama and ready to fight if need be. Mich wouldn't even look at me.

They continued to berate my wife and I still couldn't believe it!

They finally left and I was so mad at that point, I had tears of frustration rolling down my cheeks. How could a few simple requests have blown up in to World War III? I just can't believe it. My wife eventually stopped crying, but she was totally distraught.

My daughter, Samantha, was about one at this time. So, that night I wrote her a letter explaining all that had happened. I guess I just needed to write out the events and have someone hear me – really hear me, even though she was only a baby. I needed to work through all the events and all the thoughts in my mind. I hadn't intended to create this big mess – especially when I was being pulled in so many different directions. I didn't have the time or energy to give to some huge emotional drama. But, I also knew that this might be the turning point for all of us. There was the chance my in-laws could have convinced my wife I really was truly a terrible person and I could lose my family.

I stayed up all Saturday night and finished off the letter at about 6:30 in the morning. As I wrote the letter, I felt a very deep peace. I encouraged my daughter to give only love and not hate - no matter what. I knew that my in-laws probably hated me (they'd said as much numerous times) but I still must love them unconditionally for my family's sake - and for my own. I'm not perfect. I'm not superman. I'm human; I'm going to make mistakes and you know what?

It's okay; it's okay to make mistakes, but it's not okay to have a meltdown or to put conditions on someone you love. That's not what I wanted my daughter to think of me. I could be a better person, even if I'd not handled this situation very well. While I still felt my anger was justified, the results were obviously a train wreck.

The essence of the letter was that if you have to choose between loving me or your grandparents, don't. Love both unconditionally.

That next week, my wife was very depressed. I was at peace, but still on the edge of exhaustion and burn out because of the hours at work. My in-laws lived an eight hour drive north from us in a place called Smooth Rock Falls, but I told my wife that the following weekend I would drive all the way up there and make this right.

I would fix it. I'm a good sales guy, so I figured I'd just find a way to make this better and get everyone back on speaking terms again. I told myself, "You created this, you will go fix it. No problem." I had no plan, but just as with my business, I leapt out on faith knowing I would come up with a plan by the time I needed it.

That week at work, I was extremely busy and tired but I knew I had to drive up north that weekend and I wasn't really looking forward to it. Still, that weekend, my wife, daughter and I all climbed into a van with Caroline's brother, Ricky, and his girlfriend and made the trek up to Smooth Rock Falls. All the way there, I kept thinking that the last thing I wanted to do was drive eight hours up and eight hours back, but it was a surprisingly wonderful trip because it was made in the right spirit - one of reconciliation.

As we traveled along, we stopped at lakes and took little breaks to get coffee or snacks and really enjoy the journey. Just prior to us arriving in the town of Smooth Rock Falls, I got an overwhelming feeling that I needed to stay somewhere other than at my in-law's that night.

I wasn't given to strong intuitive feelings most of the time, but this time it was truly overwhelming. Smooth Rock Falls is a small town and so there isn't a vast selection of hotels. In fact, there is the Moose Motel and that's about it.

Now believe me, the Moose Motel is exactly what it sounds like – not exactly the Ritz of Northern Ontario. It's frequented by hunters and other travelers who are largely visiting family or enjoying the wilderness in some fashion.

When I shared my plan with everyone, that I was going to stay at the Moose Motel, they were all so confused that they stopped the van to discuss if this was the best course of action. We had come all this way for me to fix this issue with my wife's parents and I'm sure they thought I was bailing out at the last second. But I had a strong feeling inside guiding me that was telling me that they needed to approach them first and let Mich and Dick read the letter I'd written as a way to open the dialogue. Then, Caroline and Ricky could come get me the next morning and I'd apologize and smooth things over. Finally, they agreed.

They dropped me off and I settled into my room. Now, there's not much to do at the Moose Motel (as you might guess) and my adrenaline was heightened in anticipation of how it would go when my in-laws read my letter. It wasn't long before I was channel surfing for lack of anything better to do.

I turned to one channel and they were discussing the universe and how we're all connected, then to another and they were talking about how we attract things into our lives. Every channel I flipped to showed some sort of deep metaphysical topic. Every single channel! It was a little spooky and I start glancing around the room wondering if I was in some sort of twilight zone. This subject matter wasn't exactly prime time fare for the residents of this small town!

You know that weird feeling when the hair on your arm stands up for no reason? It was like that. I was a little panicked

It said that I'd be taking a trip soon and, when the time came, I had to follow. I've tried to describe the voice and it's almost like hearing it inside your head more so than out loud, but let me tell you – it got my attention. The closest thing I could compare it to is in the movie, Field of Dreams, the voice says, "If you build it and they will come." I didn't share it with anyone. Not that I didn't' think about it, but what would I have said, that I'm hearing voices now? The truth is I did hear it, but there was no way to share that experience without a straight jacket somewhere in my future, so I kept it to myself.

I wondered what the voice meant and why it came to me like that. What connection did it have to fixing this problem with the family and what would be required of me? Needless to say, I was thrilled to be back in my own bed at the end of the weekend, but even then I knew the voice would be back. I fell asleep wondering if maybe a nightlight might be a good idea - just in case.

Okay, I know what you're thinking, because I thought it too. Are you nuts? Here I am, all alone, in the lavish Moose Motel and then some voice speaks to me and tells me I have to go on a trip? The voice did not tell me where or when, just that I had to and that, when it was time, I must follow. Was this some sick mental scavenger hunt where I was going to be given clues right up to the front door of the loony bin? Was I about to be led into the wilderness to roam for 40 years – which would never happen because I'd be eaten by a bear or killed by a moose within the hour - this was Northern Ontario after all! Was I overstressed? Having a nervous breakdown? Sleepwalking with my eyes open? What??

I listened for a few minutes. I didn't talk, or move a muscle, I just listened. The voice stopped, so I turned off the TV, kept the lights on and got in bed – eyes wide open. I tried to sleep, but I'd shut my eyes for a minute and they'd pop open again.

Honestly, I half expected Jesus to be standing there in the middle of the room at some point. Who else could give a message that scary and cryptic? At least I was grateful I hadn't needed a burning bush; that would have really freaked me out – although, I'll admit if his image had just shown up on a piece of toast at breakfast, it wouldn't have had near the impact.

There is nothing like hearing a voice to make you reevaluate your idea of sanity. Eventually, I did fall asleep and then woke the next day to wait for my wife and Ricky to come and get me. When they arrived at the hotel, they said that the change in Mich and Dick was a miracle. I couldn't believe it; I hadn't even gone to talk to them yet – all I did was write a letter. I had to see it for myself and as soon as we got there, people were very emotional and hugging. Dick said, "I'm sorry, we misinterpreted the whole thing." Then he hugged me, which surprised me more than the apology. He's a real tough guy, not a hugger. I was as astonished as my wife and brother-in-law were. Just one week earlier, they were never going to step foot in our house or see my family ever again and now it was miraculously fixed.

All the way back, I turned the events over in my head. It was like the most bizarre road trip I'd ever been on. The whole way back, that experience in the hotel kept jumping into my mind. I didn't share it with anyone.

Chapter 2

Hitting the Wall

as I couldn't understand what the hell was going on. That's when I heard it for the first time – the voice. It was soft at first, but I know I heard it and it wasn't just a feeling – I heard a voice.

The next week or so went by without real incident. Everything went pretty much back to some semblance of normal. I was working hard and business was booming just like I had envisioned it would. We were working long hours and even weekends, so there wasn't much time to sit and ponder the great existential questions of life.

During those days, I could barely tell you up from down and ran around trying to get everything done like a mouse in a maze. I could barely order lunch, let alone consider things as deep as the connectedness of the universe.

But in my mind it had to be good, right? After all, this was the goal I'd focused on and longed for. We were making it and money was rolling in. So why did it feel so soul numbing? Not only was I not getting any joy out of our success, I felt I was being drained by a pack of vampire bats - with huge appetites.

The days slipped back into routine and then, only a week or so later, on Sunday, I was at work for about 12 hours. I was so tired and physically exhausted that I couldn't even begin to think straight, so I walked across the street to a little grassy area where I had some privacy, curled up in a ball and tried to sleep. But, it's hard to sleep when it is 50 degrees out! Still, the exhaustion was all consuming.

On Monday, I kicked my feet off the side of the bed and sat up. The dawn had just started to break with purples and pinks. I just sat there and slowly dropped my head into my hands. I was so tired, the kind of tired when you know you are finished and can't go on one minute more.

It wasn't like lying down and getting an extra hour of sleep would have mattered because the kind of exhaustion that filled me was the kind that you know will destroy everything you ever tried to be.

I just sat there desperately trying to think of what to do. Next thing you know, I was weeping –definitely not something in my normal morning routine, but certainly one of the signs of complete burnout. I knew I couldn't go on, but had no idea what to do next.

My body was breaking down and at that pace I knew I didn't have much time left. I was sad and knew that deep down I had been muscling the universe, meaning that I had been using all my force of will to make things happen and I was getting what I was asking for as far as increased sales. But the problem was that I had failed to picture the harmony to go along with it, so eventually I became so completely drained that I had barely managed to keep myself together. But now it was over. I just couldn't do it anymore. I had no idea what direction to go and no idea if I could even take another step.

My mind wandered back to that experience at the Moose Motel and I'll admit to being a little frustrated. There's nothing like a voice popping into your life and saying you must follow. Where is the freakin' voice now that I really needed some direction? I felt all alone and desperately miserable.

Needless to say, my wife was very upset and who could blame her? There's nothing like waking up at the crack of dawn to find your husband in a weepy puddle on the floor. She knew I was breaking down physically and emotionally.

So I tried (very poorly I might add) to pull myself together into some semblance of manliness and get out of the house and off to work. In my mind, I had to go to work. Work was on fire after all and we had so much business that I felt I had to be there no matter what. So, I drove off down the road with tears in my eyes wondering, how in the world I would make it through the day.

When I got to work, it was pretty obvious from the reaction of some of my coworkers that I wasn't hiding my problems as effectively as I thought I was.

I had spent a great deal of time with these people – more than with my family at that time - and they could see I was emotionally distraught. It was clear to everyone I was tired, but they were tired too.

I thought I was hiding things well before, but I know they probably knew something was up for a while. You can hide certain things, but you can't hide the fact that you're one stop away from needing heavy-duty professional help.

Now I knew that sleep wasn't helping me anymore. Physical sleep was not doing it. I knew I was in crisis. Something had to change. When I went into the plant, people stayed away from me. It's almost like when you're a child and you see your father crying. It's very disturbing. I was still weepy, so I went and found a quiet corner of the plant where I could be alone.

It was early morning, about 6:30 am, and the plant was 26,000 square feet, so it wasn't hard to find a spot to be alone. I remember saying that I just couldn't do it and began crying again. That's when I said out loud, "I will go anywhere and do anything to find out what the answer to life really is. I will go anywhere and do anything, just show me the way." That moment was the second time I heard the voice.

The voice said, "Okay, it's time. Let's go. Get in your car."

I thought, "What do you mean go? Just like that? I can't just leave!"

The voice said, "GET IN YOUR CAR".

I thought, "I don't have anything to lose." I decided right then to do what the voice said.

I had to tell my business partners something. I couldn't in good conscious just disappear and leave them holding the bag with all the business we had going on, not to mention the fact that almost everyone in the organization had seen me teary eyed already and knew something was up - which was very awkward. I finally ended up telling them that I thought I had a drinking problem and had to go somewhere to recover. I know it was a cop out; I also knew that was something they could understand and wouldn't question. However, if I had started the conversation with, "there's this voice, see, and it said....", then they would have driven me to the mental hospital themselves!

My brother-in-law –Rick – also worked at the plant and found me pretty quickly. He got the fact that I had to go, but wanted to know exactly where I was going. He knew Caroline had no idea what was going on.

The good thing was that he knew some of the deeper struggles I was having and so I could share some of the details with him. I told him that this was more about figuring out who I was and the spiritual side of things. I also told him I just had to go and had no idea when I'd be back. That's when he got very concerned and told me to call home. I had a wife and small child and he thought maybe I was running out on everything. I told him the same thing I'd told my partners, that I had a drinking problem and had to recover. I didn't tell him I heard a voice. I made my excuses to everyone. Then I left.

The second I left that building, got in my car and started to drive, I felt like I had more energy than I've ever had in my life. It wasn't like nervous energy, but the kind that fills you with peace – and it had been literally years since I'd felt anything like it. It was an absolute peaceful, tranquil calm like you can't imagine. It was unbelievable bliss and joy and peace all at once when just moments before I'd been a traumatized ball of exhaustion.

I got back to the house around 9:30 am and no one was home. Usually, by this time of day, I would have had three or four cups of coffee and eaten something just to keep going. Strangely, though, I wasn't hungry or thirsty and yet had tremendous energy.

Again, I questioned the whole idea of following the voice. I really had no idea where I was going, so I wasn't even sure what to pack. A line from "The Godfather" popped into my head, "Leave the gun. Take the cannoli." It made me chuckle a little because I felt on the verge of a great adventure. The voice kept urging me to get in the car and have faith. Why was I suddenly so happy, peaceful and full of energy?

I packed my guitar case, my music, all the books I had been studying, clothes and anything else I thought I'd need. I spent probably an hour and a half reveling at who I was at this time.

It was surreal, like time was standing still. I was by myself and able to think, to notice things around me and look forward to something. It had been so long since I'd felt that way and I'd missed the experience of living in the moment.

I got back in the car and drove south, toward the states. I didn't really have a specific idea where I might end up; I just had the urging to go south – and I did. It was spring (April) in Canada and, as I drove south, the trees and flowers became more and more beautiful.

I went through Buffalo, NY and every once in a while I'd stop just to enjoy seeing the splendor of the world. There was a feeling of connectedness - that I was at the right place at the right time, doing the right thing and that there was something great for me to discover along the way.

Remember what it was like when you were a kid and your parents took you a road trip?

You noticed everything: the cars passing by, the houses, the scenery and it was all new and different from what you'd left behind. That is how it felt – almost a childlike awareness of all that I'd been missing in my daily routine.

Once I got on the road, I wasn't worried about what, where, when or how this trip would unfold. I knew that I was going to the perfect place at the perfect time to get the perfect message – whatever it was. I also knew that if I would just follow with faith and love, I was going to be okay.

The calm was unbelievable. I was totally relaxed, totally happy and unbelievably full of energy. The weight I had been carrying had exhausted me and now that it had been lifted, I was bubbling with enthusiasm for life. It seemed almost impossible and I even wondered if I was going to have a 'real' breakdown somewhere down the road because just that morning I'd been so exhausted that I'd almost collapsed.

Somewhere around 6:00 pm that evening, I drove into the outskirts of Columbus, Ohio and realized that I hadn't had anything to eat or drink all day. But I still wasn't hungry or thirsty. Nor was I tired. If you had told me a short 24 hours earlier that I'd feel completely rejuvenated without any sleep or food, I would have thought YOU were the crazy one. But, that's how it happened. At that point, the rational part of my mind decided to stop and get some kind of sustenance just in case I got hungry later.

I bought an apple and an orange and sat them on the seat next to me. I still had not eaten or drank anything that day, but it didn't matter.

I drove into the night and don't even remember all the names of the little places I passed through. Somewhere between midnight and 1:00 am – about 16 hours since I'd left the plant - I stopped and got out of the car. I was still not thirsty, hungry, or tired.

By now, I was getting a little concerned. What's going on? I kept looking at my hands and making a fist and looking at my body trying to figure out what was happening. That's when I realized there were no cars on that road. I was all by myself on an interstate between Cincinnati and Louisville that should have had some traffic, even at that hour. But there was nothing but an empty expanse of road stretching into the darkness in each direction. There were no clouds; it was a clear night. Yet, all I saw was a full moon and two stars aligned to the West. I kept rubbing my eyes thinking, "Okay… there have to be more stars if there are no clouds." I stood there for a good fifteen minutes, but there were still just those two stars pointing west. Then I got nervous.

I was standing on an interstate all by myself in the dark hundreds of miles from home. My mind flashed to an old episode of The Twilight Zone that started out this way and I know it didn't end well! So, I got back in the car.

I have to think that those two stars were a sign that I was going in the right direction. At least, that's how I took it. My rational mind was telling me it was one in the morning and I needed to sleep even if I wasn't sleepy.

There were a few hotels on one side of the road that were nice, but of course they were all full for the night. Then I went to the other side of the highway to a not-so-nice hotel, which was a little mom and pop.

The sign in the lobby read "God loves you". I was totally content and full of peace and joy. I went to my room and, for the second time in 2 weeks, slept with the lights on. That may sound a little surprising, but my mind just couldn't really grasp the whole chain of events.

I didn't know how I could go from being that sick and exhausted to this total awareness about who I was and where I was at this moment.

It was almost like an experiment, with me as the guinea pig, and yet I felt at one with everything. It's tough to explain.

My rational mind, however, did work to explain things, so I started to think that any minute Jesus would appear, which is why I had the lights on. If he showed up, I wanted to see it! Yes, this is the most rational explanation my mind could create. I knew I wasn't about to die, so Jesus had to be on his way. I was a little nervous and I paced for a while. I finally lay down and closed my eyes.

Not even five hours later at, 6:00 am or so in the morning, I awoke totally refreshed, totally at peace, still not hungry, not thirsty, nothing. That's bizarre because I normally couldn't quite function without a few hundred cups of coffee. I got up and drove all the next day, winding my way westward. That morning was when I figured out I'd been carrying around my guitar case with no guitar! I had to laugh. I was thinking that it was as it was meant to be; I could just pick up another guitar. Maybe Jesus did show up last night and he swiped my guitar! I laughed for quite a while and it struck me that I didn't remember really laughing like that for a long time. It felt good, like my soul had just been released from death row.

As I continued to drive, I ended up turning into a little town not too far off the interstate in Missouri. One of the first places I saw was this little music store and it was great.

I went in and bought a 12 string Ibanez to put in my empty guitar case. I had never tuned a 12 string guitar, so the guy there taught me to do it. It was a wonderful time.

For the first time in years, I didn't have anywhere to be or anyone to answer to and I could immerse myself in an experience as small as tuning a guitar and have it be meaningful. I kept driving and that same surreal sense of peace followed along as I went. It was almost like this was the first time I'd really done anything for myself of significance.

That year, 1995, was the year of the Oklahoma City Bombing. In fact, it had just happened about 30 days prior to me driving into Oklahoma City on this trip. I took some time and walked around Oklahoma City and the emotion there was so unbelievable. I remember it being so quiet, almost reverent. I went to the site of the bombing and there were people crying and walking the streets.

My problems, in comparison, seemed so small. Those people were going to work and conducting their daily routine just like I did every day, but now they were gone and I was still here. What did that mean? For whatever reason, my guide, this entity that directed my travel, had wanted me to see and experience that sadness. I didn't understand it at the time, but I've come to realize that it was important for me to have that experience. I had overwhelming feelings that I felt there and that emotion highlighted the urgency that I had to figure out what was in store for me and what message I was there to receive.

Years ago, I had so enjoyed music. It was a refuge for me and gave me a spiritual uplift at times. Over the years, though, I had less and less time for it. Now, I felt that I wanted to take my new guitar and play in a canyon; just be one with the wilderness and the creative energy I felt surging up in me. Sounds a little crazy I know, but then so does driving across a continent because a voice said so, so I went with it.

About 20 minutes outside of Oklahoma City, I passed just the right place. I went up to a nearby house and asked the lady if I could just walk on her property and play guitar a little.

I'm sure she thought I was completely deranged or some kind of weed-smoking hippie, but she said yes anyway and so I did. I just sat there and strummed the guitar and released the sadness I'd experienced in Oklahoma City and connected to that wonderful peaceful state.

I was soon back on the road again and headed through Amarillo, Texas finally stopping at a little town just inside New Mexico. They call New Mexico the land of enchantment and it certainly is. I knew by then I was heading to Santa Fe. It was an intuitive knowing; the voice hadn't said anything, but I knew that was my destination. This was my last stop before arriving in Santa Fe and this little motel that I stopped at was really strange. When I checked in, the guy greeted me said, "My name is Bud and I'm a Buddhist monk."

Okay, I thought. I said, "My name is Joe and I'm a Canadian drunk." I like to keep things light after all. Bud had some really bizarre concepts about life. He thought that the U.S. government was giving machine guns to inner city blacks to create gangs in all the inner cities so that someday they could oppress the people of the United States. So, I listened to this, trying to mesh this idea of his with the fact that he said he was a Buddhist Monk. Bud was convinced he was the only one who knew about this conspiracy in this little town too! He was a funny, strange guy.

That particular night, however, my experience in my room was very different. For the past couple of days, I'd had this beautiful, tranquil surreal feeling. But that night, it left me for the first time since I'd left home. I went to bed and I turned out the lights thinking, okay, tonight I'm going to be a big boy and sleep with the lights off and a very bizarre darkness came to me. It was as if there was something evil in the hotel room, or the hotel, and I experienced that evil presence. I know it sounds strange, but there was something not right about the place and

I felt it to my very core.

Intuitively, I was guided to walk across the room and put on some music.

Instantaneously, I was back in that peaceful state and felt like I was protected. I knew I was going to be safe that night. I had a very, very deep and peaceful sleep. I realized that the second I did what I was intuitively thinking, I went back into that state of tranquil peace. It was almost a lesson in trusting my intuition, which I needed because I was certainly out of practice.

The change in me in just those two days was dramatic. I had been completely exhausted when I left Ontario and only had five hours sleep last night and the night before. I had driven over 3500 km, but I felt so calm and relaxed. I had this tremendous energy just vibrating through every part of me. I wanted to see and experience everything, to soak up the feeling my soul had been desperately crying out for. I wanted to create music and embrace whatever was in store for me in Santa Fe.

I didn't know it then, but Santa Fe means 'city of faith' and that was what it would be for me.

Chapter 3

Santa Fe

I rolled into Santa Fe about noon on Wednesday. Having never been there, it looked like something out of a movie set to me, with all its buildings and businesses, even convenience stores, made of adobe.

The rich red dirt and surrounding mountains gave the air a crisp, dry coolness and it was almost as if I could hear the drumbeats of ancient Indian tribes. I found a hotel near the historic downtown area and checked in. I couldn't wait to get out and walk around, taking in the sights. The trees were leafing out and desert spring flowers dotted an arroyo that runs near downtown with color.

I breathed deeply of the clear, clean air and had an incredible peaceful awareness as I walked through the historic square and past The Inn of the Governors.

People milled about the streets, both tourists and locals, but the area had a serene vibe, almost as if the rest of the world didn't exist. I felt connected to that place right there in that moment and my mind drank in every sight and every experience.

I had an intuitive feeling that I was supposed to go to a place called The Light Institute that was in a small town named Galisteo, just outside of Santa Fe.

The Light Institute provides techniques to get in touch with your inner self (such as past life regressions) and that is what this whole trip was about, so it made sense. I drove out to this facility and the people I spoke to told me that they are booked months in advance, but to come back the next day and if they had a cancellation they could get me in. I wasn't worried at all. I knew there would be a place for me, so I drove back to town.

On the way back, I thought about how significant this trip was for me and felt as if I should be recording it somehow.

I have a friend in Toronto who is heavily into photography and also owned a company that does infomercials and various television projects. He is a very spiritual guy, so I called him and gave him a brief overview of this spiritual journey I was on. I asked him if he could come and record it via photos. Unfortunately, he couldn't, so I was a little disappointed because I felt as though he was suppose to be the one to record what was going on.

I hung up and, a few minutes later, walked down a back alley toward a tiny little tea room. Now I have to say that, at that time, I was not a big tea drinker – at all, really – but it seemed like the right thing for that moment, so I stopped in and had a cup. I was the only man in the place, but I sat at a little table and just enjoyed the peace and serenity. A few minutes later, a man stomped in and began to hassle the woman who was the owner.

I became clear they were getting a divorce and it was a little messy. He verbally attacked her until I finally got up and separated them. He left and the owner was grateful. We got to chatting and it turns out that she was a world class photographer who'd even had her work displayed in the Smithsonian. Within minutes of meeting this woman for the first time, she said that she would follow me around and document, via photographs, this spiritual journey I was on. One door closes and the universe opens up a window!

It seemed that, all along my journey, I met the right people at the right time and was in the right place for everything to come together and show me what I desperately needed and wanted to know: What is the essence of life? I knew with each step, each experience, that I was closer than ever to understanding.

I think one of the lessons that really became relevant to me is that you many think your good is coming from a specific direction or source when it's actually coming from a different place. Your job isn't to dictate to the universe how your good is going to come to you, but rather just to know that your good is going to come. That is your only obligation as the co-creator of your life, to hold the picture and belief that you'll get the answer.

I believed that I would be going to the Light Institute the next day and that there would be a place for me. I also believed that some person would somehow record my journey. Within the hour, we're talking 60 minutes, I got a person who was not just willing to take pictures, but was also a world-class photographer. I was at the right place at the right time, but it was even more than that. We don't dictate to the universe; we just put our intentions out there and allow it to flow to us from any direction.

The next morning, I went back to the Light Institute and, of course, they'd had a cancellation and I was able to jump into the program. They focus everything on you discovering you; it's not any kind of group therapy or anything like that. It's all about connecting to your real self, who you are underneath all the illusion of life. There are four days that each consist of two (four hour) sessions.

Each participant enters a small, private room and you lay on a table much like a massage table. It is comfortable, but modest and there are no distractions. Then they do something called 'opening windows to the sky'. They do this mostly through touching the top of your head. I didn't really realize it at the time, but what they were doing is helping me open my chakras, or energy centers, to clear out the negative things that are blocking that universal connection and allow the energy to pour through my body. Ancient eastern beliefs include the idea that we enter our bodies through our cranium and then that energy flows down our spine to inhabit the body. Our spirits respond to that energy while we live and, when we die, our soul leaves via the same avenue.

At the Light Institute, they take you through past life regressions to help you understand who you were and what you did in past lives. It is a process to see how everything is connected – the past, the present and the future.

Now before you shut this book and think I've gone nuts, let me say this: I do believe that our souls never die. It makes sense to me. After all, why would God go to the trouble of creating a soul in his image if it didn't go on after the body dies?

Actually, most religious or spiritual people also believe that our souls don't die. They may believe those souls go to 'heaven' for eternity according to their religious beliefs, but I believe that our souls have the need to try again. We go through this life and we have many different experiences – all of them perfect, all of them perfectly valuable to our journey. Some people are much farther along on their spiritual path than others, but I think we get as many chances for our souls to experience and grow as we need and once our life is passed, we can come back and experience even more growth.

The Light Institute mediator took me through the process of seeing my own birth, which was a moving and emotional experience, and also through a couple of my past life experiences. I can say that I am glad that I wasn't anyone like Abraham Lincoln or someone that had some sort of notoriety or celebrity. The process came easy for me, I think, because of my attitude going in. Remember that I'd promised I'd go anywhere, do anything and listen to anyone – and this was definitely a unique experience! But I opened myself up to it without judgment. I had asked for guidance and I just wanted to find the essence of life and what it all meant. It didn't matter that it was very different from what I had ever experienced and very different from my Catholic upbringing.

I was following my heart, which led me to the Light Institute, I think, just to show me that, hey, you have past lives. I didn't need to be told that our souls live multiple times.

I believe it wholeheartedly. That is a tremendous source of joy for me. The mediator, Pat, was kind enough to guide me through the sessions. She was a wonderful lady and we laughed and laughed. The atmosphere was very loving and peaceful.

The second day I went to the Light Institute, I decided to park my car by this beautiful little hotel. I haven't stayed at it, but it was one that was a typical rustic ranch-type house. It probably was an old ranch at one point, but now it's been converted it into a hotel. It was beautiful and had a texture to it that was almost like stepping back into an old western, where everything happens at the hacienda.

It wasn't just plaster and drywall like so many places are these days. They are mere shells, but this place had a presence about it. I decided to walk through a little arroyo next to the hotel before the session. I guess there could have been rattlesnakes or any number of things out there, but I didn't care. I was living in the moment and it just felt right. I was what the Buddhists call being 'mindful' or hyper-aware of the energy and things around me.

After a few minutes of walking, I looked down and there was a huge eagle feather on the ground. I knew it was special the minute I touched it, as if it connected me to the Indians who had lived here. I took it back with me to the Light Institute.

I was so aware of my surroundings and so aware of my connection to everything as I walked through nature. I passed a couple of horses that were standing about 50 feet away and they both stared at me almost expectantly. I knew that in this kind of mindful state, I could communicate with animals. I don't know how I knew; I just knew. We're all one. So I tested myself and gave them a command. I told them to move to their right.

The horses moved to the right. I told them move back and the horses moved back. They never broke their gaze from mine.

Now I realize that it could have been a coincidence, but I don't think so. It was a real 'oh my God' experience for me and I walked right over to those horses and just patted them. Nothing more, nothing wild, just patted them. It was as if it was tangible proof of what I was feeling and I needed it. I needed to see something so extraordinary that I couldn't pass it off.

I think we're all like that to some extent. We can go and have a great, life altering experience somewhere, but then we start passing off that experience as less than great in our own minds. We can't hold onto it. Those horses obeying my commands may not have been a big deal to anyone else, but it was huge for me.

There was no denying that something beyond my own understanding was happening and I knew that I would just accept what came, no matter what.

I went back and the instructor asked if I knew the significance of an eagle feather to the Indians. I said, "Yes, that they tell a story." I said this, not because I knew that, but because the feather had impressed a story on me. I completed my sessions and they revealed a couple of things to me.

When I saw my past lives, they came to me in flashes. In one, I was a Native American Indian a few hundred years before in the same area I was now visiting. I was one of the people in charge of the tribe. I was a warrior, able to keep and protect my people and to find food. One day, I left with some other warriors and, when I came back, our people were gone, most of them slaughtered by soldiers. I then spent the rest of that life wandering around, searching for peace because I was alone. Yet, more than that, I felt tremendous sorrow and sadness for those that had died. I felt I had let my people down.

That experience really relates honestly to the feeling that I had within my own business in the present.

I would empathize tremendously for my employees. I worked

hard - very hard - and was driven not just to earn more for myself, but because so many people's lives depended on me. At one point, we added a bakery business to our core business and there was a time it was on the verge of going down. None of the employees knew it, but that's really why I worked so many hours and was so involved. The easiest thing for me to do would have been to let it go, to just step back and say, "I tried but it's done."

I couldn't do that. Those people had families, dreams and aspirations that would have been devastated if their livelihood had disappeared. I knew because of the experience of this past life that I felt a tremendous need not to let anyone down again and in this life I refused to just let it go.

The other life that I experienced was one in which I was some kind of an entertainer. I can see remnants of that in my present life as I did stand-up comedy as a kid in Toronto and had never had a problem getting up in front of people – never. It's not totally in me to go out on the road and perform, but I can do it easily and I enjoy doing it. I think that in another life, for sure, that's what I used to do. So, of course, I'd be comfortable being on stage.

The sessions themselves were very emotionally draining and after each four hour session, I might stay in the room for another hour or hour and a half just to rest and gather my strength. It's an interesting experience to be so totally at peace that you can hardly stand up!

But that's what it was. It was a tremendous self-quest and there are some people that like that sort of thing and some that don't. I loved it. It was very, very beautiful and quiet. I wasn't distracted with anything or anyone; I was just trying to understand what makes Joe tick on the deepest level.

I was sleeping very well at this point (with the lights off!) and I awoke each morning with tremendous energy that gained more and more strength. The day after my last session at the Light Institute, I awoke and saw a woman in my room clothed in a long emerald gown. To be honest, I don't know if I saw her in that time of twilight sleep before I was fully awake or if the image was really in my room but it was that real. She didn't say a word, but when I got up, I knew I was going somewhere and it had to do with this woman. The voice was back and told me to get dressed and go. I listened.

Once out the door, it was as if there was a GPS device in my ear saying, "Turn left; turn right; turn left." I walked and walked, but I was just following the voice. It was like working in a coal mine with no idea what is in front of you. I don't know how far I walked, but it seemed like a long time. I thought about what all had happened, how the voice had guided me, how I was suddenly not tired when I'd started out exhausted and on the verge of a total breakdown. The sessions at the Light Institute had begun my understanding that everything is connected and I was about to learn how to make that connection work in my life.

I also understand how those guys that sit in a lotus position in a meditative state for 18 hours do it; you don't even notice your physical body when you are completely in tune and at peace.

Of course, it's a good thing that I didn't have to sit that way because I might still be there! I'm not the most flexible guy in the world, but walking I could handle.

Every once in a while I'd wonder, "How much farther?" I'd just question it and have a little fun. There is a large school for the deaf in Santa Fe, just off of Cerrillos Road. When I got there, I knew something was up. I saw a bunch of people and they were walking into the auditorium, so I followed them. I knew when I stepped inside that I was in the right place.

There was no sign out front and I had no idea what kind of function I was attending, I just knew I was supposed to be here.

Everyone was quiet and then, after about 15 minutes, the lady from my dream came out onto the stage in a long white gown, got into the lotus position and started to meditate. She meditated about 20 minutes/half an hour and still there was absolute silence, so I had no clue as to why I was there or what this even was. I thought I was coming here to learn something profound, but no one was talking! How was I supposed to learn if no one said anything? I know that I communicated with a couple of horses, but people are a whole different deal.

Suddenly, she placed her hands together (what they call Satsang - basically a gathering of people to talk/meditate on spiritual topics). People started to pass the microphone around, talk about their issues and ask the lady on the stage questions.

One woman grabbed the microphone and said, "I don't understand. I'm in darkness all the time and I'm so scared; I'm so scared. I'm just so afraid and I can't get out of the darkness." The next person took the microphone and said, "I'm not at peace. I'm not and I don't understand why. I want to know when my peace is going to begin, so can you tell me?" The next guy said, "I'm reading, reading and reading all these books and I'm trying to understand, but I'm just not getting it." I listened and as they talked; I realized I knew the answers. Not the superficial or placating kind of answers, but the real answers.

They passed the microphone to me. I told them a bit of my story, about what had happened that led me to this journey. I explained that the voice told me I was supposed to go on a trip. I didn't know where I was going and ended up here, at whatever this happened to be, because I didn't know what it was. Some people in the audience started to cry.

Then, I started answering the questions. I said to the lady that was in darkness, "The answer's obvious - walk into the light, walk into who you are."

To the person who was not at peace, I told her that I had experienced peace on this trip and that my thousand years of peace had just started. I said, "Only you can tell you when your peace will start. You and no one else."

To the guy who's reading all those books, I said, "Sometimes you have to just put the books down and revel in the essence that is you, the Self within the self."

That's when the lady on the stage said, "Satsang" and she got up and left. Everyone started leaving. "Way to clear a place," I thought. It was kind of interesting that they all came to see this lady and she didn't say anything.

I couldn't help thinking that all these people came to learn how to listen to themselves and that they tried doing this at the school for the deaf. The lady sent someone afterward to say she wanted to speak with me. I told that person about my dream, but that the woman had been in an emerald green dress. She said, "Normally she wears green, but today she wore white." I knew that it wasn't meant for me to talk with this woman; there were other things I needed to do. Following the voice, I just left and went on about the rest of my day.

I explored Santa Fe, which is just a beautiful town. I explored parks and went to art shops - and you know there are a lot of art shops! The city has so many unusual and unique places and I was drawn to experience them. For a few days, I just walked around and enjoyed myself. One day, I was in an art shop and met a guy by the name of Ken Peterson who turned out to be one of the guys who worked with Walt Disney to help create The Walt Disney Company.

I bought some of his artwork, though I didn't know it was his. He turned to me and said, "Thanks for supporting me." We hit it off and he was a great guy with unbelievable stories about Walt Disney. The photographer that was following me around took pictures of us and Ken invited us both to dinner.

We went to his place, just outside of Santa Fe, and his house was filled with incredible art. I could listen to Ken for hours on end. He gave me a book, his most prized possession, *The Edinburgh & Dore Lectures* by Thomas Troward.

That copy was underlined, emphasized and written in, with notes saying this is what Walt believes, this is how Walt built Walt Disney and many other things. It is a very interesting book as it talks about the scientific basis of why we do what we do and how we can connect ourselves to this universal power.

Meditation – that's what Satsang is, the union of your soul to yourself and now I was being shown that there are scientific ways to do it. I was being shown that what you put out comes back to you. Like the idea of Karma, if you put out love and goodness then that is what you get in return. Walt Disney believed that wholeheartedly and so do I. This trip was the first time I'd completely surrendered to the idea that I needed to connect to something beyond who I thought I was.

I know a lot of people accomplish great things with seeming ease, while others struggle just to keep their head above water. In my mind, the universe was showing me there was a better way, an easier way, a more fulfilling way to live. I had already tried to do it all myself and force what I wanted to happen on circumstances and people. It almost killed me and my effort still only took me so far. I understood that I had to surrender all the ideas of what I was and who I was in order to discover the bigger and better life that awaited me.

Each encounter I had in Santa Fe was another step in that direction, even though at the time I didn't necessarily put everything together. The important thing was that I opened myself up to whatever was in store and then surrendered to the experience even when I had no clue what it was or what was happening.

While I was in Santa Fe, it seemed that every single person I came into contact with had a smile on their face and was glowing with happiness. Life was easy. Magnificent. People were loving. No kidding! Looking back on it, it was the universe demonstrating the fact that everything I was experiencing was just a reflection of me.

I was happy and at peace and that is what I got from others. At home, before I left, I had been difficult and hard to get along with sometimes because I was worried and stressed and bearing the weight of many on my shoulders. This trip taught me that that the stress was my doing. I gave out stress and guess what I got back? Yep. More stress! It was a reflection of me and had nothing to do with the circumstance. Everyone you meet in your life and the circumstances you create are a reflection of you. So the reflection should reflect something loving. If you look in the mirror and don't like the reflection, you don't change the mirror, you change you.

I was sending out not just bad thoughts, but thoughts about making $2 million a year and I was always pissed off because of something, whether it was the traffic, the sales numbers or the family. I was just angry. I didn't realize that I wasn't controlling my thoughts and, therefore, I was sending out more negative thoughts, which brought more and more chaos into my life. I created the circumstances that justified the negative thoughts. That's exactly what happens. You create circumstances that justify the thoughts within and you get emotionally attached to that circumstance and give off the exact vibe that you don't want.

That's why it's important to control your thoughts in those moments when you have anger. Don't suppress the anger. Instead, invite it in and thank the anger for teaching you how not to act, then just let things go. Change your thoughts or you'll create exactly what you don't want.

I think back to the incident with my in-laws and realize they were reflecting my own negative thoughts. It had nothing to do with them; it was and always will be my responsibility - 100%. That reflection was probably one of the biggest gifts they could have given me in my life, if not the biggest, because it sent me on the journey that changed my life. So, just like my high-school teacher who said I was a waste of space and that I should quit because I would never amount to anything, it was a great gift because I would remember those words and they spurred me on. I now can easily say that I love that teacher with all my heart and feel nothing but love for him. He helped make my life great.

He was not saying those words to me; I was saying them to me. Please hear and feel the meaning of what I just said. You are 100% responsible 100% of the time for what is transpiring in your life. Do not give away your happiness to anyone or anything else but you.

During this trip, I did stay in touch with my family. I would call home every other day and ask how they were. I'd say, "I'm okay. I'm coming home pretty soon" and told them not to worry. I think they were just relieved that I hadn't put my hair into dreds and started smoking peyote!

They could hear that I was at peace and definitely better than when I left, but there were a couple of times I had to get my dad on the phone because he thought maybe I should be committed to a sanitarium. Taking this trip is not what he would have done; he didn't understand.

I said, "I know you don't understand, but it's not for you to understand. I'm going to come home and it'll be alright." So then he was fine. But I understand his perception.

How does your son get up and leave a baby and a wife at home with no explanation and drive off into the sunset without saying anything to anyone? I had to go through this by myself, as everyone has to go through things by themselves at certain points in their life. My father and mother have been my greatest teachers and I could not have asked for better parents or better guides.

But, ultimately, we must all learn our lessons our way in our own time, to have the experiences we came here to have. I spent a little over a week in Santa Fe.

Now I was totally at peace and the voice told me it's time to go. I packed and got back in the car, then decided to go back a different route. I thought I'd go up through Colorado, Chicago and through Michigan versus back through Texas, Missouri, Kentucky and Ohio. As was true the whole time in Santa Fe, every night was filled with new information for me as I discovered more and more about my inner self. I wrote over 40 songs and wrote hours of comedy.

Many of the songs revealed my thoughts and emotions so clearly, yet I'd been hard pressed to express those feelings and ideas in my normal life. Songwriting gave me that creative outlet I needed and captured much of the raw emotions I went through.

Because I was so in tune, I wrote them down as fast as I could. I wrote some of the humor that I saw in things that happened as well as some of the information I was learning about life.

This was an evolution for me because I wasn't really a 'write it down' kind of guy, but I knew this was a life changing time and I was compelled to write it all down.

Every single night, I played music for hours and hours on end then contemplated life, only to go to bed at midnight and get up at five and do it again. This continued from the beginning through the entire trip home.

I didn't think about what awaited me at home. I was living in the present, just having a series of 'now' moments. I was completely at peace as I drove. I headed up toward Colorado Springs. From Santa Fe, it's about a five-hour drive or so. I was used to driving 14 or 16 hours in a day, so suddenly the voice was telling me to stop in Colorado Springs and I actually had the nerve to argue! I kept thinking, "I'm not tired. I don't want to stop." And the voice kept saying, "Yeah, you've got to stop. You're staying here tonight." And I'd say, "No, let me go further. I can go another four or five hours easy."

I know; after all I'd experienced, I had no business arguing with the voice. It hadn't turned out well before, but I'm stubborn like that. Then it started to rain. Not a little drip rain, but tropical downpour rain. The voice kept saying, "You have to stop." As I was saying, "I'm not stopping", it started raining harder and harder to the point that it was ridiculous. I might as well of had a fireman's hose on my car.

When I couldn't see the road in front of me anymore, I gave it up and agreed. I took the first off-ramp I saw and noticed that the road I came to was "Garden of the Gods" Road.

It made me laugh out loud. I went under the overpass and sat in the parking lot of a hotel. I didn't get out of the car it was raining so hard. I just waited for the voice. It's not like I was in a rush at that point, so what difference did it make if I sat there a minute?

The rain stopped and I went to check in. There were two ladies at the front desk and their names were Hope and Faith – honest to God. I thought it was a joke; pouring rain, Garden of the Gods Road, Faith and Hope working at the hotel.

Someone's having a little fun with Joe. I thought something really interesting must be in store for me tonight.

The next morning dawned and you know what had happened that night? Nothing. Absolutely nothing. I was confused, I thought, "Wait a second. I did what I was told and got off the road and stayed at the special hotel and now, nothing. Fine." So I packed up to leave. My nature is to get up early and get on the road, so I headed back down to the highway. I got to the interstate and needed to turn right. The voice said, "Turn left".

I said, "No, the highway is to the right."

The voice said, "No, you're turning left."

I stopped dead in the road. I was not a happy camper. First, it tells me to get off the highway and stay the night and nothing happens. Now it was telling me to turn left when I need to go right. My nature said, "Now we're going home. I'm supposed to go home, what the hell am I doing anyway?" So, I finally do as it says and turn left and then a couple stop lights up, I turn left, and turn left again and that's when I said to myself, "If I turn left a few more times, I'm going to do a full circle and then I'll really be pissed off!" It would be annoying to hear the voice say "recalculating" because it drove me in circles.

I was in a residential area when I stopped the car. I didn't want to get out. I knew this voice was going to make me go up to some stranger's house and I didn't want to. But I did.

I went to the house indicated and knocked on the front door. I heard a lady say, "Come in." I walked into this tiny house and she was in the kitchen calling for me to join her there. As I entered the kitchen, the house seemed to be thousands of square feet instead of tiny. I noticed that the rest of the house was filled with angel artwork all over the place.

The woman said, "Hey, how's it going? You want a tea?" She didn't know me from Adam, but acted as if she expected me and that all this was completely normal. I figured I might as well have some tea with her. As we drank our tea, I realized that this was a lesson in guidance. I had listened to the voice and to my own intuition, but I didn't really know what was guiding me. That's when the universe told me –angels.

Angels have been depicted as guides throughout our history. I knew I was guided and could be guided. We are all guided, even if you don't understand or believe you are. But in order to tap into the real power of that guidance, you have to understand two things: first, you have to believe that you are guided and then you have to ask. I had asked to be guided on this quest and I had been (even though I'd fought it at times). I had been a little frustrated when I didn't see the 'why' of things, but, with patience, the reasons and lessons were revealed. Religious people ask for guidance all the time, be it from Jesus or Buddha or whoever they believe their spiritual guide to be – and they get that guidance based on their belief.

I thought about that all the way home. I had asked to find the essence of life and that request had been fulfilled. The essence of life is finding and understanding the self within the self – who you really are without all the illusions and assumptions we gather along the way. Then, create with all the love and joy you can. Enjoy the journey; enjoy the experiences; enjoy getting to know yourself. My journey to Santa Fe had come to an end, but my real discoveries were just beginning.

Chapter 4

The Illusion

I arrived home from Santa Fe and was greeted with quite a bit of excitement from friends and family. I'm sure many of them were just relieved I had returned and not disappeared completely. Others just seemed to look me over as if expecting a second head to sprout. They would ask things like, "Where'd you go?" And "What did you do?"

I honestly didn't know exactly what to say. My heart was bursting with this life-changing experience, but I was afraid if I started sharing even part of it that they would quickly commit me to the nearest funny farm. It's hard to keep that kind of excitement stuffed inside, but I did it and soon life went back to the same routine. Well, the routine was the same, but I was definitely different. I was in a great state of peace and the stress I'd experienced before, as well as the exhaustion, was gone. It was if I could somehow shield myself from all those things that grabbed at my soul and threatened to destroy me before.

I'd made a pure and heartfelt connection to something bigger than myself and that connection allowed me to exist in a space outside the illusion I'd created for my own new life. I've mentioned this illusion before, but I think it bears discussing in depth here. When I say 'illusion,' what I am referring to is the fact that we all create our lives – good or bad – and that creation often then takes over. We start to believe that we must behave a certain way, believe a certain way and think a certain way. But there are no rules that state that you must do, say or be anything.

We end up constraining our own lives down to the size of box that we imagine we should have. We get an idea that we are the kind of person that ___________(fill in the blank). It might be that we can only earn a certain amount of money, vacation in certain types of places or even marry a certain kind of person.

We put all kinds of ridiculous restraints and restrictions on who and what we are before we have any clue as to what our actual potential is.

We become emotionally attached to things that just don't matter and we fear their loss when losing those things we are unnaturally attached to might be the best thing that ever happened. We are not humans having a spiritual experience; we are spirits having a human experience.

Take my experience for example. I had created a life with a young family, a growing business and all the trappings of what some might think of as a great life. Then, I got crushed by my own illusion. I was carrying the weight of the world around and burning my candle at both ends. Something had to give – and it was the illusion that had to go. I'm not here to earn a lot of money; I'm here to experience lessons in the school of life.

I can honestly agree that I got a crash course on a bunch of lessons that were needed for the development of my soul! I had to disconnect from all the 'stuff' and reconnect to something bigger. That sense of peace was worth more than any money in the bank or any trappings of success ever could be.

Now, prior to this, I will tell you that I would have been the last person to sit by a stream in the Lotus position and connect with my inner self. But after that experience in Santa Fe, sign me up! I realized that only by surrendering could I move forward. I had to let go and move forward on faith – and it worked.

Now that I was home, of course this big, earth shaking experience slammed right up against that illusion that I'd created. Not only had I created the illusion of who I was and how I behaved in my own mind, but all those around me were also used to a certain version of me.

Because I didn't know what to say (and had that fear about wearing a straightjacket the rest of my life!), I held back a lot of what had happened. Most of the people around me, especially those I worked with, thought I'd just had a great vacation because I was so much more relaxed and rested.

That was fine with me because I was focused on staying in that place of peace and connectedness.

Understand that not everyone will be supportive of any type of change in your life and there have been many people through the ages who have been ridiculed for their beliefs, especially when there was a vast change in the direction of their lives. I know some people, even some who have known me most of my life, will read this and say, "That Joe's a nut bar!" But that's okay. This is my reality and I know what truth it holds for me and my life. It's not about other people. Self-discovery is all about exploring within and finding your path to peace and happiness. No one can tell you what will make you happy and no one can make you happy. It comes from inside and I think we all know that on some level. We choose our own happiness or not and nothing in the external world can make that choice for us. We also choose to face new challenges with peace and openness or with stress and dread.

Almost as soon as I returned, our business took off like a bottle rocket. Sales soared and we expanded as fast as we could breathe. I stopped drinking and started taking care of myself, not only spiritually, but physically as well. My wife and I soon had another child, a son, and we were just motoring down the road of life. Everything seemed so much easier. I went from those long dark days before Santa Fe to a harmonious existence and I have to say I was happy. I realized my mood wasn't dictated by circumstance anymore; every circumstance was just an illusion anyway. In fact, it was the other way around; my attitude and overall mood affected everyone and everything around me.

Work was much more pleasant as the people around me caught a little bit of the peace I felt. It happens by energy osmosis! That means that when we spend time around a happy, peaceful person we can start to feel some of that happiness seep into our lives.

The people around me didn't change; I changed and that was the catalyst to create a great environment where we could really get things done without a lot of struggle or tension.

Now I still had a grumpy, negative business partner but you know, it just didn't bother me like it had before. He taught me a great lesson of how not to treat people and how not to bottle up anger and hate inside.

He was living his own reality and his own illusion and it made me sadder than anything that he chose the kind of fearful, unhappy life that held little hope for peace at all. I'm sure you know people in your own life that are like this. No matter how beautiful the day, they are convinced the sky is falling and the rest of the world is just too stupid to notice.

I don't have an innocent view of the world by any means, but I do know that there is a wonderful existence out there for each of us, so when I see someone purposely throwing it away it's hard to believe. I have never been, and will never be, the kind of person who tries to convince anyone to think the way I do. I don't know everything; in fact, I just know what I've experienced and if that experience can help any one person, then I'm happy with that. I leave everyone to their own discoveries and experiences and that's how I treated this partner. We saw each other daily and I focused on giving nothing but love to everyone I met, no matter how negative they were. I don't know if I made much of an impression on him, but I can sleep easily at night knowing I tried to be the best version of me that I could be and I hope he benefited from that somehow.

One interesting thing that happens when you come off the emotional high of a life-altering experience is that it's hard to fit yourself back into a 'normal' life. But I did and I hid much of what I learned and believed. When you hide, you eventually get worn down day by day and slowly life slips back largely to the way things were. You lose the connection and that is what happened to me.

I heard Bob Proctor say, "Once you have it made, you have to keep it made." In other words, if I had come back from Santa Fe and just really gone into that deep connection, I wouldn't have lost it. In fact, I would have enhanced the experience and grown exponentially.

But I didn't; I went back to a "normal" life and just worked on being more harmonious in my visualization, but I didn't work on the connection to my inner self that I had experienced in Santa Fe.

Once you have it made, you have to keep it made. That's what I was told and that's where I screwed up (we are always in the perfect place at the perfect time, so when I say 'screwed up,' I mean that it is for me to learn to keep trying to make the connection today and forever - we never really screw up).

At the time, I was just going off the high of the experience, kind of like an adrenaline high. I wasn't regularly connecting to myself and to that greater power on a consistent basis. So, over time, that feeling faded. I wasn't meditating for the connection. I was visualizing for my business and my personal life, but I wasn't going about getting what I wanted in the most effective way. I was grateful for my life and for other things, but I got wrapped up in that illusion again of having a booming business, great house, wonderful vacations and the perfect family. I thought, "If you do this life over and over again and you never die, what does it matter if you are a saint or not? I should just enjoy life."

Instead of saying "I want to make a connection to get direction for my soul first and foremost," I got wrapped up in the superficial again. That was a big miss for me because my whole journey started with me finally giving in and asking for direction and I was given that perfect, divine direction. Now, when things were going well, I wasn't asking for direction; I was taking over. I was getting caught up in my own illusion again, caught up in all the 'stuff' of life instead of focusing on the connection to my soul.

This is easy to do when your life is good and you seemingly have all that you asked for.

I was given this gift of life experience and because, deep down, I'm a loving person to begin with, that went a long way, so that sense of peace and happiness didn't leave overnight. I was reading books and studying the metaphysical aspects of life and various laws of attracting the life you want. Intuitively, I was more in touch. But, like with many other things, you start making compromises and then, before you know it, you are caught up in your own illusion again.

I feel that we're here to learn and progress our souls. To make a connection, one of the ways is to meditate. During perfect meditation, you are moving closer to who you are.

The closer you are, the more intuitive you get. The further away you get from your true self, the more distractions fill your life (things like drugs and alcohol, anger and fear). You might think that if you create your reality, then what does it matter how spiritual you are? Can't you just focus on riches and be done with it?

Yes, you can focus on wealth if you want. I've been there, done that and I just about lost my mind. So, for me, that route just isn't worth it. You're either going one way or the other in this life because there is no status quo and the other way's not good.

It is your choice, but there is supreme peace to be found, so why would you intentionally choose chaos? It is much more beneficial to strive toward this connection with God or a universal power.

Remember that life isn't a destination, it's a journey. Yes, I wanted to create a great life for myself. That's what started me on my journey; having money or not having money wasn't the answer. In fact, once I finally made that connection, money came easier than ever before, but it wasn't the money that changed me. That change came from inside.

As we started growing the business and I got caught back in that illusion, I just got busy. I started to compromise and set aside what was important for what was urgent. For example, over the years after I left Santa Fe I also lost my desire to play the guitar. Music had been such a heavy and integral part of my spiritual journey, yet I'd set it aside and didn't even want to go back to it. It wasn't sudden; it was a slow progression that I didn't really notice and it was, in a way, reflective of my distance from that feeling of connection.

Thirteen years later, the voice came back, telling me to write a book about my spiritual experiences. It took me three years of arguing with the voice to finally listen and the text you are reading right now is the result of that. I had to overcome the feelings of unworthiness I had.

I thought that either I wasn't the kind of person that writes a book or that, if I did, no one would read it. I haven't lived a pristine life and I've made more than my share of mistakes.

I finally realized that it doesn't matter if anyone ever reads this book because this journey is about my personal growth. It doesn't matter if people think I'm crazy because, again, I'm conveying the ideas that were shown to me. Writing this book was all about staring into the face of my own fears and taking action instead of letting them convince me it couldn't be done.

The message for me has nothing to do with the money and success in businesses, although logic would say that I should have written a business book just because I've been successful in that area. But I don't want to get caught in that illusion. Money and success aren't the real goal; the connection is, the journey is. More than likely, I'll never experience something like my Santa Fe experience again in my lifetime, but it was a privilege to have it happen at least once in my life. It was unbelievable, in fact, and it happened to ME! Now, I've been told to write so I know I have nothing to lose and perhaps everything to gain.

The Art of Connection

Since I resigned myself to writing this book I slowly made my way back to that connection and even moved to a deeper and more meaningful connection each and every day. I want you to be able to experience this yourself, so I am going to walk you through a typical day for me and show you what I do to connect. There are infinite ways to do this and my way is just one which continues to continuously evolve.

The first thing that I do is to start each morning, as soon as I get up, with appreciation and gratefulness. These two emotions are powerful and give you the opportunity to stop anything negative right in its tracks. I am appreciative for the day, for who I am and that there is a self within myself. I recognize who I am apart from the current illusion of my life.

I acknowledge and recognize myself for who I am and I am thankful. That's huge. People don't realize the power in gratitude and thankfulness and how they can alter your perception of events during your whole day for the better.

Once I express my gratitude, I try to meditate sometime in the morning, if at all possible. I'm at the stage in my life where most days that is possible but some days it is not, so I don't. My life is not in perfect harmony every second of every day, but it is in much greater harmony than it was five years ago and I hope to be in even greater harmony still five years from now. I don't strive for some strange illusion of perfection and I also try not to beat myself up about anything.

There are some times that I clearly regress, but that is okay because it just means I have more work to do on myself. Like anything, the longer I can meditate, the better. Typically, I like to meditate for between 15 minutes and 30 minutes in the morning and then one other time during the day - sometimes just before bed. It allows me to get into that state that Buddhists call 'mindfulness'.

You are more aware and intuitive about the things that happen through the day when you are mindful. You also connect with that feeling of peace as you allow the concerns of the day wash away. I have read many books on meditation and would highly recommend that you find out more about this tool and the incredible power of connection.

Connecting, for me, is getting my mind to a state that is the absence of thought, which is difficult to do. This is especially hard for me, because when I meditate now, I get thoughts of what I should do today or next week with a particular project. So, I think whenever you're connecting to yourself in a meditative way and clearing your mind, you're able to then listen to the voice that's within and able to be guided.

Meditating can take many forms. It has changed for me and probably will keep changing for the rest of my life. The bottom line is that meditating is the act of consciously controlling your mind, however you choose to make that happen. You've got to control your breath and you've got to control tension within your body by relaxing.

You can picture our bodies with an antenna while you are trying to meditate. If your antenna isn't up, then you're probably not going be able to get good reception. It's very critical that your spine is aligned because of chakras, or power sources, within the base of your spine and the top of your head.

Align your spine vertically, not slumped in your chair or lying down to get the most benefit.

Start by taking a deep breath. Breathe through your nostrils as much as you can and then release that breath fully. You should have a longer exhale than inhale. When you finally release it completely, imagine yourself relaxed and getting a massage on the beach listening to the rhythm of the waves go in and out.

Focus on that sound, in and out – and continue to breathe.

You will start to relax and calm down. Now, you must get hold of those racing thoughts, about how many emails are in your inbox or what you have to accomplish right after work. Let that go. Our minds are very powerful and this can be difficult for some people. You may find it effective to have a recording of a noise (like ocean waves or trickling water) to focus on and clear your mind. This need to focus is why you hear some people make sounds or chant. They are focusing on the sound and clearing their minds. Buddhists do their chants in words, but you can do it with any sound you like. You just do it repeatedly and what you are doing is putting yourself under hypnosis.

Have you ever seen anyone put under hypnosis? The hypnotist says, " Close your eyes, relax" and then they start to relax the person with their words. Once they get you to repeat their meditation they can influence your subconscious mind. You're doing the same thing, but to yourself.

Now before you say, "I'm not doing that!" Let me say that there are many roads up the mountain. I mean that there is no 'right' or 'wrong' way to meditate, as long as you make your own personal connection. For this reason, you have to find what works for you and that means trying out a few options before you settle on one. You can be a Hindu, a Catholic, a Buddhist or an atheist.

If you want to believe in a supreme, infinite power rather than say the word God, which is what I do, that is fine and how you meditate to connect with that power is completely up to you. I only mention what has worked for me and know it could change. I'm always trying new things and I keep an open mind to the various ways to connect better to that infinite power.

There are some that don't even sit at all when they meditate. They do something called 'mindful walking'. This means they walk slowly with their hands clasped behind them.

They go very slowly and focus on connecting within themselves and their surroundings.

One vital element in making a connection is to ask for guidance. You must surrender everything in order to gain anything and this is true in connecting each and every day. You release the illusion you are living and wait for direction to move ahead. The ideas of thankfulness, gratitude and asking; asking for Jesus or Buddha or God or whomever you want to be guided by, to come into your life and show you the way to make the connection stronger. Some Christians call this 'Christ Consciousness,' meditating on the Christ Consciousness.

Don't worry about getting it perfect. The important point is to move ahead because progress is progress and making that connection is vital to your progression. You make some kind of connection whether you want to or not, so you might as well understand how to affect it to make the perfect connection and create the perfect life for yourself.

At the very least, you will be pointing yourself in a positive direction rather than a negative one and that alone can change your life. You can experience bliss, joy and love and those are wonderful feelings.

At the end of the day, any kind of meditation is better than no meditation, so even if you have just a few minutes, you can still achieve a relaxed state. You can start by controlling your breathing, maybe holding your breath a little bit before releasing it.

There's so many different ways to practice controlled breathing.

But all you are basically doing is seeing yourself relaxed, then imagining every part of your body as the tension drains away from them. At the same time, clear your mind of thoughts to allow the space for that connection. This is a quick mini-meditative state that you can do in five minutes at lunch or even in your car right before work.

It's important to point out as well that, once you start meditating, your meditation grows and changes just like you do.

So, you may start out in a very primitive, or simple, state of meditation, but as you grow and learn, you become able to connect faster and hold on to that connection longer.

As you grow, your connection gets stronger and you become able to define your life more. I love the saying that it's okay to be you because everyone else is taken. Some days are good, some not so much, but as you continue to strive for connection and peace, it grows.

We're creating karma every minute, which is why it is so important to give only love. Those things (emotions, feelings, actions) go out and they're going to come back. If you give love every second of every day, within a short period of time, you're not going to have anything come back that won't justify love. But it's not that easy to do. In fact, it's very difficult.

For example, let's say you get into a situation: someone broke into the house downstairs and they're robbing you.

There's panic, fear and anger - all these emotions that you send shooting out into the universe that are coming back to justify you and you justify them. But this is detrimental. Meditation gives you the ability to ground yourself and control your thoughts. It is the most difficult thing you will ever learn to do.

The toughest thing we will probably ever have to do is to control our minds and make the connection on an ongoing basis that brings us more joy and peace and love – a happier life. Sending thoughts of peace and joy to someone else is right.

Anger, doubt, fear, jealousy and envy - those emotions are all indications that your thoughts are not in a positive place. Be thankful when they appear in your life. It's another opportunity to overcome them with love.

I know some people journal what comes to them during a meditation session. In some cases, it's a reinforcement of what they're supposed to be doing. We are all aligning with what we think we're supposed to be doing down here in this incarnation. We progress in this lifetime so long as we can get back to a connection.

Will I make the connection perfectly in this lifetime? I don't know. I can't tell you that, but I can tell you this: I'm not going to stop trying and it won't be for lack of effort on my part.

To summarize:

Reflection (thankfulness, gratitude)

Connection (mediation to connect to the Self within the Self)

Direction (inspiration on how to live your life)

Perfection (now you are living a divinely guided, loving life)

Reflection ➡ Connection ➡ Direction ➡ Perfection

Chapter 5

The Elephant in the Room

I've been dancing around the idea of spirituality versus religion so far in this book, but now it's time to address the elephant in the room.

What is God? I'm sure you've noticed that I have referred to the universal consciousness as God several times throughout this text, but I don't use the word 'God' in the traditionally accepted sense.

We all grow up with the idea (from organized religions) that God is a grey-haired man in long, white robes that is happy when we do good and punishes us when we do wrong. I grew up thinking this just as most young people do. I was raised Catholic and was even an altar boy. My uncle is a priest and I have two aunts that are nuns.

I don't disparage their beliefs, but I've come to believe something slightly different. This doesn't mean that I want less than religion has to offer; it's that I believe there is more available to us than can be defined by the strict confines of 'religion' as we know it.

I believe that religions were developed to help regular people, like you and me, understand something so grand and so big that it is literally incomprehensible. The idea that we are all connected and have the ability to change any way we want at any time we want is decidedly God-like from my view.

I don't think we were created in God's physical image – so, no, I don't think there is an old grey-haired man watching me from a cloud. Instead, I believe we were created in God's mental image.

We were given the ability to connect to a universal consciousness emotionally and this gives us untold power over our lives.

Religions created by men can't even begin to really understand the complexity and power that this entails, so they try to interpret it the best way they know how – by creating sets of rules and ideals intended to make it simple. Some of the rules are for control.

The problem is that it's not a simple concept to grasp and that's a good thing because we have to work at it. By striving for more than we can comprehend, we get closer and closer to living in that consciousness all the time. I believe that there have been many individuals who have walked this earth who were living in a connected way all the time.

They were very far along in their soul's journey. These are people like Jesus, Buddha, Gandhi, Mother Teresa and many others. We have the urge to deify some of these individuals because those around them at the time recognized that they had an understanding and connection to this greater power that was far from ordinary.

Sometimes when I see a very pious religious person who rejects my ideas, I have to step back and realize that they are just caught up in their own God delusion.

I don't mean this in a derogatory way; I just know that they are limiting their own understanding by trying to force their idea of God on a universal power that is so much more.

I want to state that I believe that if your trip is to be a Catholic, Hindu, Muslim, Jewish, Buddhist or to have any type of religious affiliation (or none at all), then you should walk that path with all your heart.

Just because it is not my belief does not make me right or wrong; it just is my belief. Remember this is a play in which we chose our own role; so, play your role with all your heart. By trying to fit God into our little box of what we have been taught God is we are not allowing ourselves to discover all the things that await us. Prior to Jesus, the faith of the people he interacted with was Jewish.

The idea of Christianity was itself a rogue idea that turned the Holy Land upside down. How then can we now say that the movement toward spirituality or divine consciousness and away from organized religion is wrong or in some way heretical? We can't.

Yes, I have been approached by those who feel that the Bible is the only truth in the universe and I agree that it holds some wonderful teachings. But the book itself was written and assembled by men. When they developed what we know as the Bible, many books and some passages were left out – including those that mentioned reincarnation. Does this mean that the idea isn't valid or Christian?

No. It means we got the edited truth, not the whole truth. The important thing is to understand that you grow in your spiritual journey in a vast number of ways and only one of those ways is participating in organized religion. But there are many more ways if we allow ourselves to be open to understanding them.

Of course, you can absolutely be a Christian and believe in a universal spiritual consciousness. God is more, not less, than we believe. Whether you do or don't actively participate in the traditional idea of religion does not matter. What matters is your ability to grow and continue to come closer to the idea that giving love returns it.

The more you move toward love and light, the more your life will show evidence of that spiritual growth.

Going to Hell

One thing I get asked a lot is if I believe there is a Hell. I can say that I absolutely do not. We are not created to be destroyed because we didn't do something perfectly. The reason we need to grow is that we aren't perfect!

We will make mistakes and can grow from them, but the additional guilt and trauma that the idea of hell evokes does not lead to positive growth. God did not create hell, men did, and it's here on earth with us each day.

We each have the ability to choose our thoughts and actions; it's called free will. This free will can be abused and often is. Some people choose to lie, cheat, steal and kill. They choose to be evil and set about creating the mayhem we all see on the news each night. There is evil in this world, but it's caused by the wrong thinking of imperfect men.

I believe that when our souls are released from this physical form, we go to the astral world and then we can choose whether to come back and have other experiences. Again, we have free will. We are not forced to stay, nor are were forced back; it is our choice. I believe that evil (no one is really evil) individuals are afforded this same choice.

They don't just disappear into some dark crack in the universe because they did evil things.

Every soul can choose redemption and, given centuries and even eons, they can find their own redemption at any time, if they but choose.

This is what I believe God is.

God is the recognition that souls never die and none were ever created to be destroyed. The universal consciousness is about love, so the idea that there is someone waiting at the pearly gates with a big sword to smite the bad souls just doesn't ring true to me.

If you think about the idea that real hell is here with us now, then you take on a different perspective. You realize how important the choices you make are and how, by taking responsibility for everything in your life (justified or not!), you can make the choices that keep you out of harm's way and on your own path to enlightenment.

Humanity is chaos; the universe is order.

So the struggle we are experiencing is how we learn and grow toward that perfect connection and that is what we are all after: that perfect experience in which we are so in tune with the universal consciousness (God) that we become one.

When you listen to sermons, what do they focus on? Usually, they are about creating that perfect closeness to God so you can go to Heaven. This is exactly the same thing. God is more than we know and heaven is us perfecting that connection to God to the point we are one and the same.

I have a lot of beliefs in common with many 'religious' people. We may differ on some details, but the main idea is the same. We all want and strive for the same things and there are many paths to get there. Mine is only one and yours is only one.

My Ancestors Were Snails

For a lot of people, the idea of reincarnation in any form really trips them up. They see various other religions that believe in reincarnation and, quite honestly, it freaks them out. I know what they are thinking, "Well, what if I come back as a cockroach or something and get zapped by a bug zapper?" I understand that and, no, I don't believe that if I see a snail creeping across the patio that it might be my great uncle!

People, again, get hung up on the physical form they might take in the instance of reincarnation, but that is not what it's about. We are forcing the idea of reincarnation into a box we can understand easily and that's all. But true reincarnation isn't about the physical body, it's about the soul.

I'm not going to say I'm any kind of expert on the subject, but I believe my soul continues when I die.

I also believe that I will return to continue learning and growing because I have experienced so much in this short life that I can't imagine it being over at some point. But our bodies do die, so there has to be another solution and the ability to live again in another body gives me another chance to give love in its truest sense and to work hard to connect more perfectly. No, I don't worry about who I might come back as – it's really kind of ridiculous if you think about it. We have free will, so why would I choose a cockroach? I would choose a form that allowed me to learn and grow the most.

I don't discuss these ideas openly very much and most of us don't, really. We don't share the deep recesses of our beliefs in the normal course of the day, even with family. In fact, many people simply choose to believe what they were taught as children. They get up every Sunday and go to church, but they never choose to really grow spiritually.

There is a quote that is attributed to Eleanor Roosevelt and it states that "Small minds discuss people; average minds discuss events; great minds discuss ideas." I like this quote for a couple of reasons. First, it describes the growth of our consciousness perfectly. We start very petty and small, but as we grow, we expand our minds to the universe and beyond.

Second, it easily details the fact that we are all at different stages of the journey. You will meet people who are mere babes on their spiritual quest and then there will be others that astound you with their insight and connectedness.

All we need worry about is our own journey. What is life all about and why are you here?

The Truth Tingle

One of the real turning points is when you understand that the journey you are on isn't about success or wealth, but about internal growth and the understanding of your true self.

You also must know that many people around you won't understand and it can drive you apart. This is okay. Things are not meant to stay the same forever because we are all moving along on our journeys at different speeds. This means that people and situations will flow in and out of your life. It is to be expected and anticipated, not feared or dreaded.

Of course, it can be difficult to know when things need to change. I've learned to pay attention to something I call my 'truth tingle'. No, it doesn't involve electricity or batteries, so don't go there. When I hear of, or experience, something that really resonates with where I am on my journey, or where I want to go, I will get a chill that runs down my spine. This is the 'truth tingle' because I know that it resonates with my spirit so closely that it causes a physical reaction. This has happened at various times in my life and now happens quite regularly, as I am in a space where I'm living in a more connected way than ever before.

As I said in the last chapter, I knew for a long time (more than three years) that I was supposed to write this book, but I resisted. I was afraid of what people would think, of the friends I'd lose and of the awkward family holidays that might ensue once it came out and people really understood what my beliefs are. But I knew that one day it would happen.

When I met up with the person that helped me corral all these ideas and get them on paper in an organized way, that tingle was back. I just knew this was the right time and the right space. Did it go exactly as I envisioned? No, it took longer than I thought, but that was me imposing time constraints on the situation. As it turned out, it unfolded exactly how it was supposed to and if that connection hadn't been there, it would have been very hard for me to get it done.

That physical resonance with a person or event has proven right 100% of the time, so now I know when it happens to surrender to what the universe has in store and allow the situation to unfold in its perfect timing. I don't limit myself or anyone else – well I TRY not to, but I'm human so it does happen on occasion. But when it happens, I remind myself that I'm stepping on my own toes and I need to get out of the way.

Opinions as Universal Chatter

"Don't care what other people think and stick to what you know to be true." Ever heard that? I have plenty of times and I've finally reached the point that I am not affected by anyone's opinion of me or what I believe. They can think whatever they chose to and I'm good with it. But, I will say that it took a long time to get to the point that it doesn't bother me – I'm over 50! We'd like to think that the opinions of others don't drastically shape and affect our lives, but they do. Oh, sure, it's because we allow it, but we all want to be liked and to get along with others so we allow their opinions to matter more than they should.

I once heard a lady ask a well-known teacher if it was Christian to believe in universal consciousness. He looked at her and said, "Why do you care what I think?" It shocked her at first, but she quickly realized his point. No matter how lofty the education or standing of a person, their opinion doesn't put constraints on what we believe. Only we can do that.

We seek approval for what we know to be true instead of having the courage to just believe. I know what this is like. For sixteen years, I hid my beliefs even as I was reading voraciously of the various religions and learning more about the ideas of connectedness and universal consciousness.

I had to choose to stop living a hidden spiritual life. I want people to know what I've discovered that has helped me on my journey toward ultimate happiness. If I kept it a secret, then it would help no one, especially me, because that would mean that while I gained knowledge, I didn't put it into full practice. The spiritual side of my life has grown and continues to grow.

It affects everything I do and say; how could I possibly hide it?

No matter your current beliefs, I urge you to seek your own truth, no matter where it might lead.

You may come to completely different conclusions than I have and that is a good thing because you will have discovered them because you looked, not because you just followed the crowd. No matter what you find, you will have discovered your true self and how to connect in your own way. That is more valuable than anything I can teach you. Only when you finally connect to the real you that lies deep within can you start to live a truly authentic, happy and loving life.

Chapter 6

The Power of Emotions

Your knowledge and understanding of your beliefs will evolve over time, just as mine have. This is good because you are growing in your understanding of your own truth. As we just discussed in the last chapter, there is really no such thing as a singular truth. We are taught patterns of beliefs, or belief systems, but these are learned from those around us and have nothing to do with our own connection or our understanding of our true self. You must discover those for yourself.

There is a big difference between being 'religious' and being connected to a universal power or God. Many, many religious people are very in tune with their connection, but others aren't. You have to realize it is a journey only you can travel. No one else can do it for you and showing up at a church every Sunday doesn't give you a pass either. You have to make that connection for yourself and choose to grow as a soul.

We all create our own truth and so we each carry different experiences that determine our path. Part of seeking your own truth is to understand your emotions and how they alter your perspective on life. I know many people get caught up in the idea, the illusion really, that it's easy for me to talk about these things because I have achieved success and wealth on a certain level. They believe that if they had that too, then all their problems would go away or be magically cured, but that is not so. Money and success don't define a person; they just reveal what that person has been previously thinking.

For example, I had a business partner that also achieved wealth and success, just as I did. But, as he gained these external things, he became very negative, fearful and angry. This is not unusual as you will often see success produce extreme behavior in people.

In truth, he always carried that tendency and the money just revealed it.

This is true in every aspect of life, from finances to relationships. External circumstances don't dictate your success in creating things such as loving relationships and money doesn't fix what is broken. If it did, no millionaires would ever divorce. Yet, they have some of the highest divorce rates as a group. It goes to show that nothing external can solve what is an internal problem.

I've been a guy that's had no money - and I've been a guy that has a lot of money. I can tell you solemnly that money does not bring you happiness. But our emotions affect what we believe to be possible and how we view our path to happiness. Since we can't control circumstances, then we must control our minds. How often do think about controlling your thoughts?

Odds are, not very often. In fact, it takes some effort to really stop and consider that we choose our thoughts. Most of the time they seem to just run through our heads of their own volition and we don't consider their impact. We are all caught up living life, so we don't step back and really contemplate the idea that we can choose something else. It's easy to get caught up in the 'life happens to you' attitude because it's much easier than taking responsibility and knowing that you created this experience.

Our thoughts have power and we can control them completely to create the life we want. That doesn't mean you can control every circumstance in your life; you can't. But you can have a tremendously positive effect on those circumstances and create something great. You are creating something either way: you either don't control your thoughts and let circumstances control you or you harness your mind to focus on what you want to create. It is all internal and up to you.

It's interesting that many people are afraid to get in touch with their real selves. They don't want to question their reality or delve in to the reasons behind their beliefs or results.

It's almost as if they believe they will discover a horrible wizard behind the curtain and not know what to do.

I've discovered that it's actually more comforting to get to know the wizard because the wizard is you!

It's the same experience that you would have walking through a dark forest at night – it would be natural to feel creeped out because your mind perceives that there is danger lurking nearby. It does this because you can't verify there's not something scary there, so your mind takes off, imagining the boogey man lurking just out of sight. During the day, that same walk wouldn't produce a second thought at all and you would be completely comfortable.

The difference between the two is perception and then the emotion we attach to that perception. The truth is we have the ability to scare ourselves senseless for no good reason and we do it all the time! When you think about going deep within yourself and discovering what makes you tick, it's natural to feel uneasy.

You don't know what you will find and so your mind conjures all sorts of possibilities that have nothing to do with anything. But when you take the time to peel back the layers of whom you really are, it is actually very comforting. You are removing the unknown and finding answers to questions you didn't even know you had. By doing this, you are creating more and more certainty and giving yourself much more control over your life. It is not something to fear, but something to embrace.

The power of the mind is one of the first and biggest discoveries most people make on their personal journey to universal connection. For many, it's literally life altering. They embrace what, to them, is a revolutionary idea – that thoughts are things and so they can create any life they choose.

Some who make this discovery walk around like they have a stick of dynamite in their pocket because they are so excited to use this tool and discover all life has in store. But others understand how powerful the mind is and still choose to set it aside and go back to the life they know.

It seems completely contrary to the obvious choice, but it is one made by the vast majority of people every day. It confounds me still, but I understand what they are struggling with. The definition of insanity is doing the same thing over and over again and expecting a different result.

I've already talked some about getting caught up in your own illusion of life and it is this illusion that haunts most people.

They see a glimpse of the possibilities, but then run smack into their own circumstances again. They see the reality of the life right now and it erases that small hope that life can be different. They don't feel powerful at that moment and they allow that emotion to convince them that they weren't born rich, aren't smart enough, tall enough or educated enough or whatever. They emotionally run away and hide by going back to the way things have always been.

This is very similar to what happened to me after I returned from Santa Fe. I didn't feel I could really share the experience with anyone and went back to 'regular' life. Over time, that feeling of connectedness vanished and I was once again searching.

The very idea that you control everything in your life is overwhelming, but it's also a bit like learning to ride a bike. You can't expect to jump on and cycle across the country. You have to practice, maybe even skin your knees a bit, while you get the hang of it but it takes focus and effort.

It seems easier to avoid the whole thing and just go back to the life you had. Though it may seem easier, it's actually leading you down a path of uncertainty and unhappiness.

When you don't take responsibility for the fact that you create everything, you are handing your life over to circumstances that you don't control and that is a freighting kind of life.

The first step to harnessing the real power in your life, your mind, is to learn to control your emotions. You can't base your actions on how you feel at a given moment because that emotion is something you created and that creation may not be serving you in a positive way. Just like your emotions may tell you that you are not in control, that is an illusion. You are in control, but you can't let those emotions overwhelm your thoughts. You must harness them by not trying to control with force, but rather by seeing them as the illusion they are and letting them go.

Just like that walk in a dark forest, if you allow your emotions to overwhelm you, the next thing you know your pulse is racing, you're breathing hard and you have the urge to run! Why? Are you really being chased?

No. You are creating the fear that is driving your panicked decisions and that is exactly what we do in real life when we don't control our thoughts. For example, have you ever had a time when your bills piled up and you felt buried? Did you lie awake at night and not see any way out? What happened? Did the world end? No. It just felt like it might. Worrying didn't change one thing; it just kept you up at night. You could have chosen to refuse to worry about it and focus on work and things that improved your life. Not only would the outcome probably have been better, but your state of mind would have been helped tremendously. This is what I'm talking about when I say we create our own reality.

Our emotions are fleeting and not always accurate, so we have to learn to harness our minds and be able to focus on what we want rather than the fears of what might happen. Yet, there are many people who reject this fact and refuse to accept that they have power over their lives.

They just give in to those temporary emotions and think, "Well, I guess I'm not supposed to be happy." You see this often with people who made a decision about a job or to marry at a young age and then they feel trapped with that situation forever. You don't ever have to live with a poor choice; you can choose to change and create a new life.

One of the most stunning things I've witnessed or experienced is the speed of change when a person decides to take the reins of his or her own life. Where your life might have rocked along relatively unchanged for a decade or even longer, suddenly each year brings you to a very different place in life. I was told the story of a woman who, at a very young age, got pregnant and married.

For ten years, she existed in a very negative and possessive relationship. Every year, on New Year 's Eve, she would sit on her back porch and think about the year. After ten years, she realized that this was not the life she was meant to live.

She had a bigger purpose and it took her a long time to work up the courage to change what had been a relatively secure and stable life for ten years.

She finally did and now each year still sits out on her porch each New Year's Eve to ponder the past year.

She is shocked and amazed at the speed at which her life has changed dramatically. She has since received two degrees, started her own business and remarried. It happened so quickly she can't even imagine what her life would have been had she stayed in that same old life.

It's an interesting fact that, once you climb the mountain, you can look back and think "Gee that wasn't that big a deal!" Yet, on the front end, facing the unknown, it can seem like an insurmountable obstacle. That is the role emotions play; they are like your own personal funhouse mirror.

They make unknown obstacles seem huge and impossible to defeat, but once you get past those same obstacles they seem much smaller and almost inconsequential. You wonder why in the hell you ever thought them to be anything more than a speed bump.

When you read a book such as this and you read my story, it may seem impossible that you could experience similar results in your own life. But you are looking in your funhouse mirror right now and I know exactly what that is like. I don't want to downplay it or push it off as nothing because I know how hard it is to change yourself. But, I also know how much control you have over the outcome and if you could only see it from this side, you wouldn't hesitate to start your journey.

Once you start learning to control and overcome your emotions, you can then start using them to help you create that life you desire. Emotions aren't all bad.

I know, especially as a guy, I was taught that emotions are not something you are supposed to show. I was taught to shake it off and get back to work, as many people are.

I actively suppressed my outward emotions for years, but my internal emotions and thoughts ran wild. They contributed to my anger and frustration issues. I would create or replay situations in my mind repeatedly until I was completely overwrought. I'm sure you've probably done that too.

Maybe you remember a time when someone really ticked you off and every time you see that person it brings back all that anger. This is what I mean by controlling negative emotions. You choose if you get angry or not and you can choose to give love instead of anger. You are in control.

When someone says, "Well I just can't help the way I feel,"

I call bullshit!

You don't want to. It's easier to be angry or disappointed, but it takes effort to let those negative emotions go and replace those emotions with peace, love and forgiveness. Here again, it takes practice and patience but you can choose and saying you can't is just an excuse to justify your negative emotions.

The great thing is that, once you start focusing on positive emotions and change, you see progress and that progress produces more positive reinforcement.

Emotions can work for us in a positive manner just as they can work against us. Emotions are actually a great thing as they allow us to get attached to our goals and pursue our passions – so it's all about learning to use them. They exist whether we want them to or not, so it's within your power to use them for good.

The greatest risk is in not taking a risk or changing; that's part of the trap. You have that security of knowing how life is going to go, but you also have the security of knowing you're going to be freakin' miserable.

You have to ask yourself, what kind of security is that? This is what happened to me in my late 20's. I went to a Bob Proctor seminar because I was looking for a way to improve my life and my finances.

Even though I didn't understand a lot of what was being shared then, I figured the worst that could happen would be that I'd start being more positive, so I really didn't have anything to lose.

But the more I read and the more I studied over the years, the more I realized that this is the right way to live.

I understood what was meant by 'thoughts are things' and

that you are a 'co-creator in your own life.' You can think of the emotion of love as if it were a pregnant mouse.

That emotion produces more positive thoughts and those thoughts produce more thoughts, growing at an exponential rate until it permeates your life and the lives of those around you.

We talked about religion in the last chapter and there is a Bible story you probably know about Job. Job did nothing wrong. In fact, he was a pretty good guy by Biblical standards. He lived a good, connected life and desired to grow as a person. What he got was the worst life could throw at anyone.

He experienced extreme personal tragedy by losing his entire family and then also lost his wealth. He had severe health problems and came to the verge of death, yet still he sought that connection with his idea of God and focused on the good in life.

Eventually, his life was fully restored, but his experience is a great example of the fact that circumstance does not define you. Job had every justification for anger, hatred, revenge and a myriad of other negative emotions. Yet, he didn't waver in his faith in the good.

There are times you will need to have faith because your emotions will work against you and try to convince you to give up. But those emotions only have power if you allow them to. You need your faith and to be able to cling to your reason for living, which is your life purpose. If you mix in a strong emotional attachment to that purpose, it will sustain you through the hard times.

I frequently talk about giving love; endless and abundant love. Love is the strongest emotion and, as such, can easily trounce negative emotions that try to get you off track.

Once you learn to connect to your inner self and then mix in the wonderful emotions of giving love, then you can listen to your voice and let it guide you.

If you do this with reckless abandon, your effort will be great, as will your results. In order to do something well, you must have that passion.

When we talk about purpose, I think a lot of people get caught up in the idea that they want to be a singer or speaker or movie star or whatever. But often it's not the work they want, it's the results. They see a successful singer and they want the lifestyle, but they don't really want the job!

So they try and fail and don't understand why. They thought they were creating their life, so it can be confusing sometimes. But the difference is that they said they wanted one thing, to sing, when they really wanted the lifestyle and those are very different desires.

You see this with college kids all the time. They think they want to be doctors or lawyers because they see people, or their parent, in that profession with nice homes, cars and a good lifestyle, but they have no idea what those jobs really entail.

So, often they earn degrees in a particular field only to find out pretty quickly that it wasn't what they thought. They make decisions and set themselves along a certain path and then they realize it's not what they wanted. They're miserable because they don't know how to get out of it.

When I was in college, I told my dad I wanted to play professional football. To his credit, he didn't laugh, but he did tell me that it would be a great idea if I took the summer and spent the whole time working out and pursuing that dream. I still had to work a job, but he said that if it was something that I really loved, I would spend the time after work or before work to follow my dream.

The truth is that I thought I wanted it, but not enough to

really put in the solid effort it would have taken.

I put in a good effort, but not at the level it would have been if I'd been really passionate about it. I wanted the lifestyle of a professional athlete, but I didn't love the sport at the level that kind of success demands.

I was passionate about starting my own business. While I was working various jobs in my twenties, I was continuously collecting ideas and figuring out how business worked.

It was just inside me and a desire I was willing to work for tirelessly. It was my passion, but it's not everyone's.

Many people think they are supposed to want to own a business because they think they will be in control; that they're the guy at the top who will reap the cushy hours and fat salary. But most don't have the passion it takes to get through all the crappy years when you are paying the secretary more than you take home.

That's okay. Not everyone can be an owner. What is important is to follow what's in your heart and do it to the best of your ability. You must have passion in order to achieve what you want and if you aren't making progress, then you have to step back and see if there is something else you want more.

I want to insert some ideas on gratitude right here because gratitude has a tremendous effect on your emotional state. I've already talked about how I start my day with gratitude. Like love, gratitude is one of the most powerful emotions. Think about it – when you are in a state of gratitude, how can you be angry?

You can't. That's the whole point and why I start my day out with gratitude. It wipes the slate clean and connects you to positive and powerful emotions right off the bat.

Now, when I say I start off with gratefulness, I don't necessarily mean a laundry list as in, "I'm grateful for the trees, the sky and so forth."

Those things are fine, but realize that the external is fleeting; the real gratitude is for the connection to my inner self and the wonderful feeling of being part of something greater than who or what I am. This is first and you have to have that connection to really feel gratitude for those external relationships and circumstance in your life because you helped create those things.

Everyone is a little different in what they are grateful for and, just like meditation, you have to find your own groove as to what feels right for you. There really isn't a right or wrong way to be grateful! I'm personally grateful for my life and for what's happened. All the things I've been able to experience in my lifetime, both good and bad, have helped create the life I have now.

I'm very fortunate. I'm grateful for my perfect health and I'm grateful for the peace and joy that I feel is inside me. It's huge. It's like your best Christmas ever! You open the biggest present in your life and think, "this is unbelievable, thank you so much." That's sort of the gratefulness that I'm talking about.

Attaching emotion to your gratitude is essential. I also know it's not the easiest thing to do sometimes. You want to be grateful for your family, friends and coworkers, but the truth is sometimes they just tick you off! That's okay.

You might not be particularly grateful for that circumstance at that moment, but you can be grateful that they are in your life to teach you lessons – even if one of those lessons is patience! This is true in every other area of life as well, so gratitude isn't some fake list of stuff you recite each morning. It's really thinking about what motivates and moves your life forward and how wonderful those things are.

Every experience can be used for the purpose of learning and growth; or, you can choose to fight the circumstance.

This is where controlling the mind is so important because you can choose to send love to a frustrating and trying situation and just the act of doing so improves, not only the actual interaction with that person, but your perspective about it and, in turn, the emotions you attach. It's not about controlling the journey of anyone else, but more the realization that they are all on their own journey and as you learn to let go, they are free to experience their own lessons.

As we learn to have an attitude of love in all areas of life, our paths become easier to navigate. Not because the hard events or circumstances go away (in fact, sometimes it seems they pile even higher), but it's because we control our emotions and learn how to create good even from the most trying situations.

Chapter 7

Growth is Experiential

The essence of life is the growth of your soul. We've already touched on this a little bit, but I want you to understand that growth is experiential. You can't just have someone tell you how things are and really understand. Let's take, for example, me writing this book.

I was told years ago that I had to write it, but I wasn't ready yet. I needed to experience more growth; I just didn't know that then. Even in the process of the writing, I've grown beyond my understanding of the way the universe works I had a few months ago, and that's how it is supposed to be. Each experience deepens your knowledge and broadens your understanding.

Life is a great big experimental laboratory for the growth of your soul. It doesn't matter who you are or what your circumstances, you either get busy attending to that growth or you don't; it's your choice.

One of the big concepts I want to deliver in this book is 'give only love,' but I understand if that idea might seem a little strange. Life seems to be made up of so much other stuff, that we frequently diminish the importance of that emotion. Yet, love is the driving force of the universe and if we get away from it, or get distracted by the illusion we are currently living, then we miss out.

I realize that this idea of a great big universal consciousness can be a little confusing because we want to trust what we see more than what we don't see. It's human nature. What we see are people all around us, each with their own personality and their own agenda, going through life in their own unique way. But we are each so much bigger than that. Remember how I said that we constrain the idea of what God is by trying to force him into a box we can understand?

We do that to the people around us as well. We are each more than our personality, our body, our emotions – in short, we are beyond what we think of as flesh and blood.

I can see your forehead wrinkling as you think, "Oh no, here he goes again into some lofty spiritual concept." And it's true; that is about to happen, but I want to show you how it applies to your life and how the understanding that we are all much more than the physical form we see can improve your life. Not too long ago, I heard about an old episode of The Oprah Winfrey Show and it was one that was being reused in her Life Class series.

This particular show had a spiritual teacher on by the name of Gary Zukav. Gary has written many books, but one of his most popular is called The Seat of the Soul, which is now more than 20 years old. He explains the idea that we are all souls in a simple and easily understandable way. On this particular show, he was helping a grieving mother understand the loss of her child – a very difficult and traumatic life experience, to say the least.

This mother had twin boys and one, named Ryan, had only lived a few days. His death devastated his mother and cast a lingering shadow over the whole family. Gary explained that, instead of focusing on Ryan and being sad that he isn't with them anymore, it was better to understand his death from the perspective of a soul with free will.

As a soul, we choose when we come to earth. We choose what form we take and we choose our experiences. In this case, this particular soul chose to come in the form of an infant boy that lived only a few days. What the mother didn't realize is that this soul chose this short time to be with her and experience existence as her son. The fact that he died after only a few days isn't more important than the idea that he came to give her the gift of his being. The mother's grief was, in effect, rejecting those gifts that Ryan's soul offered to her.

By clinging to the loss, she was cheating her surviving son out of the fullness of life because each milestone would be tainted by her emotions of hurt and loss for the missing son – a terrible burden for any living child to carry.

I loved his explanation because it was so simple, yet touched on an idea so vast. When we can view our lives from the perspective that we are souls that are way beyond what happens in our daily experience, it lessens the emotional impact of our struggles.

We understand that our main goal on this earth is to experience the growth of our soul through various lessons and to use the gifts we have to help others and the overall consciousness of the planet. It doesn't matter if that time is short or long and, since we know we can return in any form at any time we choose, it dramatically lessens the sting of illness, tragedy or even the greatest illusion of them all - death.

We can understand that each soul chooses and it was simply the choice of that soul to return to perfect peace and harmony at that time and they will stay there until they choose to return.

This universal power our souls return to seeks to expand and create through us, so we are co-creators in the life we experience each day and the lessons we learn. In this present form, we are a part of this power, yet separate. We are fragmented from it, but we can come back to it.

Let's assume my one mission here was to deliver this book. Let's just say that's my purpose in life. It took me 50 years to get to it and understand what I needed to do, but I'm finally fulfilling that purpose. That's why I've come. I have to deliver this one message and that's my reason for being.

Of course the next obvious question is: then what? If I've fulfilled my purpose, what else is there?

There is an overall, bigger meaning to my reason for being and that is to ultimately end my own pain and struggle by making that connection to the universal power as strong as possible because that allows me to achieve the maximum growth possible while I'm here.

That includes improving, not only my own connection to this power, but improving the lives of others and that's a big reason for being. But this is what is inside of me. We are all different, so your journey will be different and unique, which is as it should be.

When people consider this idea of having many lives and experiencing growth, then coming back and learning more, they tend to think of the process in a very linear fashion – like a staircase. You come here, live one life, take one step, then leave. Then you come back, live one life, take one step, then leave. But, it's not that simple. Sometimes a soul chooses to come back simply to help another soul grow. I believe that was the case with the death of baby Ryan. He was here such as short time; he experienced little personal growth, if any, as a soul in human form. But in the larger improvement of the overall consciousness, he moved the journey of all those lives he touched forward in their own search for connection. This contributed to the ultimate growth of his soul. When we give to others, we naturally grow in spirit.

Every soul incarnates for the growth of their soul by going through different experiences. Someone may want to know how to overcome anger and experience forgiveness, so he chooses a family where there is a great deal of anger and even abuse. If he can achieve growth in these areas in his lifetime, there is tremendous advancement for his soul because of the difficulty of the situation. Everyone in his life chooses to help him with his experience and play the different roles needed to learn or not learn the lesson chosen (free will).

So, when the life is over they will all meet in the astral world to analyze what went right, wrong and what is needed for the next incarnation - if there is to be one.

This kind of idea drives engineers nuts, but the universe isn't connected with straight lines, like Tinker Toys. It is a vast array of incomprehensible (with the conscious mind) connection and once we realize that we won't understand it all, we can surrender to our experience today and learn as much as we can. By accepting the fact that we are ultimate creators, we can accept 100% responsibility in our lives.

That includes relationships, finances, experiences and responses to trauma and you must accept that there is no one to blame but you. Your experience does not really have anything to do with anyone else around you – they are an illusion that you have created. Your experience is all about your internal growth and the circumstance you are creating will reveal whether you are getting closer, or further, away from the source.

Using this power of love, and the knowledge that you are the creative force in your life, there are two things that you must do. First, you must find your life purpose and perform it to the best of your ability, utilizing the gifts you have brought to earth with you. Second, because we are all tied together at the highest level, you must also seek to improve the consciousness of the world as a whole. Both of these things can, and should, transpire simultaneously in this lifetime.

The Christ Mind

Now it's time to talk about Christ. Yes, that Christ. Jesus, the man and the soul. I believe that Christ chose to come to earth as we each do, but his soul was much further along in the growth process; to the point of being one with the larger universal consciousness in a perfect way. He was one with the infinite, yet still had a mission to accomplish.

When his soul arrived in human form, his goal was to be the savior of the world, to give the world this ultimate example of faith. If the power of faith he had was put on a scale of 1 to10 then he had a 10! He was saving the human race; what else could there be?

When you get emotionally attached to your life's purpose, you have the power to create the ultimate outcome. Christ was emotionally attached to all the faith and all the love the power of his universal connection would allow - and that was massive. He carried that love for everybody, even for the people who were killing him.

He asked that they be forgiven, for they had no idea what they were doing. He could have created a different outcome at any point or any moment, but he chose to experience the outcome that was his physical death and rejoin the vast universal power (God) once again. Many of the world's greatest teachers have shown this same outlook toward their lives and deaths. They are focused on the power beyond the illusion we experience as this life and have a mission far beyond what we can actually comprehend.

When I hear people talk about the 'Christ Mind,' I often feel as if they just don't get it. They get bogged down in the Bible and focus on the actions that Jesus took. Then, they try to emulate those actions. This, in itself, isn't necessarily bad; it's just misguided because the true message of Christ's life isn't in the daily life he lived. It is in the connection he showed to the universal power on a continuous basis.

He showed us that, no matter the circumstances that occur, that connection allows you to create the solution to any issue. He fed five-thousand on five fishes and two loaves of bread. He turned water into wine. He walked on water in the midst of a terrible storm. These actions are often referred to as miracles, which means they are something beyond our ability to achieve. But that's not true.

Each day that we connect to our true spirit and create our lives, we are making our own miracles. There is a particular story where Jesus talked about the fact that if we only had faith the size of a tiny mustard seed we could move mountains. He wasn't just using some kind of ridiculous extreme example.

He was stating the truth. We have no idea the amount of power that would flow through us if we released all our belief systems and relied on nothing more than our connection. As it is now, if you step off a tall building, you believe you will fall. That is your belief system (and mine!). There is almost nothing that will ever convince you any different.

If we had a true 'Christ Mind,' we would understand that everything, even death, is an illusion. We would have the faith to step out and know we would not fall to our death. But, we don't have that type of faith yet and must come back to this life to grow toward that idea. Each day we choose to make that connection, we are strengthening our bond with that universal consciousness and it is that power that sustains us, no matter the circumstances.

The White Flag

So what took me so long to figure this out? I've asked myself that many, many times. It wasn't for lack of searching, which the Santa Fe trip proved. I wanted the answer, but I wasn't really ready to surrender. Now, when most people think of surrendering it holds a negative connotation. But what I'm talking about here is surrendering your will and accepting that there is a power with a better way out there.

I'm reminded of my kids when they first learned to put a puzzle together. As a parent, you stand aside and watch them struggle as they try one piece after another to get a fit. You know how to help them, but you also know that it is the struggle that will benefit them the most in understanding the lesson.

When we exist in this life, we are like that kid with a puzzle. Some people get it quickly and move on, others struggle and struggle to find their way. Some give up and don't even try. They are caught up in the illusion of their lives and are so emotionally attached the past or the future that they can't learn the lessons they need to learn in the present.

Living in the present is a novel concept for most people, but dogs understand and live it. When you think about it, a dog doesn't worry about what happened yesterday or even an hour ago. They don't sit around and worry about death or how old they are in dog years or if their upper lip is starting to sag.

They enjoy lying in the sun the same today as yesterday, reveling in the experience. This is the kind of surrender I'm talking about: surrendering your worry, your past hurts and grudges, and existing in a spirit of love and forgiveness each and every day.

We can get so caught up in our own human imperfection that we feel almost trapped in our lives. Learning to let go is a skill like any other and can be learned. When you hold onto past events, you make them bigger than they ever were and you relive the emotion attached to them.

Remember when I said that to truly connect to your inner self and create your perfect connection you had to become emotionally involved? So, what then does it mean when you are living negative past events repeatedly in your life? You are separating yourself even further from that connection we all so long for. One solution is to forgive, but that means forgiving yourself and others as well.

This comes up a lot when I talk about being 100% responsible for your life, 100% of the time. In order to do that, you have to acknowledge that you created that life and it is very hard to accept that if you have had a lot of bad experiences.

But, eventually, you learn that those bad experiences pushed your own growth forward to this larger understanding that you might not have if your life had been easier.

It's time to wave that white flag and stop trying to control everyone and everything in your life. All you can control is you and that is more than enough. In fact, it is everything! When you surrender your idea of what life is supposed to be or how things are supposed to happen, you open yourself up to so much more than you ever imagined possible.

You are not defined by the events in your life and you are not the sum total of what people see. You are more than that and you will continue to exist far beyond this life. That makes it so easy to give the kind of love that really means something.

Surrender was messy for me. I felt the first glimpse of what that looked like when I took the trip to Santa Fe.

I literally surrendered to the experience and received so much awareness and knowledge that I had no idea I even needed. Of course, it was just a glimpse. I didn't understand these concepts at all back then and have spent literally thousands of hours since studying and learning ways to help recreate that connection.

Part of that was full surrender to what I knew to be true and in alignment with my own soul. That was the messy part. Some of my family and friend relationships changed and, while some people saw those changes as negative, I know that they are just moving into a different phase of connection.

Some are improved, some are not; but the bottom line is that I am experiencing personal growth on a tremendous scale now that I have raised my own white flag and surrendered to all the knowledge and understanding this existence has in store for me.

I can say with certainty that raising your white flag starts with forgiveness - for the past, for yourself and for those in your life. When you live in a state of love and forgiveness, you resist the urge to take on any new hurts or be affected by circumstance.

This new perspective is the one thing that will free you from your current prison of stress and unhappiness. It's not some big mystery, but it requires consistent action on your part to make that connection each day.

I Deserve a Bucket List

One of the fabulous things about this life is that we can go and experience some truly life changing things. Many people have a 'bucket list,' which is a list of things they would like to see or experience before they die.

Often, these are intriguing and wonderful adventures, but you have to wonder: if someone has a bucket list, what is it that keeps them from checking off all the things on that list? One of the biggest issues for many people is this idea of deservedness.

We all come into this world penniless and naked and we go out the same way, but for some reason we have certain belief systems that help convince us that we can't have good things or experience wonderful events because we aren't good enough. Sometimes these belief systems come from past experiences, or negative events, but they can also be ingrained by formal religion.

I recently talked to a friend who said she'd visited a church for the first time in years. The first thing that was asked of the congregation was for them to stand and recite over and over "I am not worthy." She was extremely upset by this and I don't blame her.

When you understand that we are all part of a perfect universal consciousness (God), then how can anyone be unworthy of anything? The answer is that we can't.

We are all worthy of whatever this life has to offer us. Our souls journeyed here through their own free will and took the form we experience now by choice. We are worthy in every way possible to experience happiness and growth. The idea that a human being of any kind would somehow belittle that is nonsense. God created us in his emotional and mental image – not as some kind of bad knockoff that can't make it to real happiness anyway.

We deserve anything and everything and we are worthy of our lives and experiences. While our souls will grow in this experience, no soul is unworthy. By the same token, there is also no person that can't choose change.

This is talked about frequently when people discuss criminals and what they call 'evil' people. There are people who revel in evil actions and I have no doubt of that, but that doesn't mean their souls are unable or unworthy of redemption. They can, at any time, choose that redemption and change will manifest itself – there is no wasted experience. Sometimes a soul's experience is all about the pain of disconnection from the ultimate source of universal power.

They experience a hell on earth and then they can choose to improve that experience the next time or not. But it has nothing to do with being unworthy or undeserving; it has to do with our choice to experience this lesson in this life for our soul's growth.

Somewhere back in our human evolution, an idea was planted. This idea was all about cause and effect, which is a solid universal law. But we have warped that idea into something we think of as fairness or worthiness. We believe that if we are 'good,' we are better than others we judge as 'bad' or that if we do X then Y will happen – the idea of Karma.

We spend a lot of time getting lost in the 'good' and 'bad' ranking system as we compare ourselves to those around us. Religion is especially good at this, as many religions actively poke holes in the beliefs of others. We want rules to live by that make things easier and we are truly a rule society. We can't even cross the street without a rule for it!

The problem is that we take this warped sense of karma and need for rules and try to apply that to our souls. But, souls need no rules. They exist in perfect harmony, waiting for us to connect and it is only when those souls choose to come back in human form that they experience intense pain and suffering.

The ideas of worthiness and earning our way to heaven were created by humans and have little to do with a true understanding of how our connection to universal consciousness works. Just knowing this allows you to put those human beliefs and ideas into perspective. What difference does it make if someone is 'bad' or 'good,' since neither affects your personal connection or ability to grow?

Here, again, it is all about viewing the big picture rather than getting caught up in the imperfection of human existence. By letting go of these old beliefs, it allows peace to come into our lives and permeate all we experience. So, if you haven't made a bucket list, do so right now. Think about all the joy you will have experiencing those items and make them happen. You deserve it.

Chapter 8

The Foundation of Love

So, what can you do right now this instant to start living a better life? All these intense, high-level concepts are great to ponder, but how do they change your life right now?

They don't. Oh, sure; having a greater understanding grows your spirit over time and that has certainly happened to me. But right now, today, you still get up every morning, go to work and then try to have a good relationship with family and friends. How do you make that better?

The title of this book is *Give Only Love*. That phrase is the key. It is the one concept that will allow you to make a positive, tangible change in how you live your life and in how those around you respond to you. You don't have to know the origin of the universe or be on some kind of spiritual quest; you can simply choose to give love. This doesn't mean that you have to wear tie-dyed shirts, hemp sandals and start handing out flowers to strangers on the street. What I'm talking about is teaching yourself to be completely present in your life right now and to consciously choose your thoughts and actions. If those thoughts and actions center around love, then your life will improve and that is a guarantee, because unconditional love allows you to be in connection with this power and you will be guided divinely.

I think before we can discuss this fully, it's important we have a good understanding of the kind of love we are talking about. There have been numerous places in this text that I've talked about the idea that in this life, you should give only love. It may sound like I am saying that if we have this love fest, then all will be well. That's not really the kind of love that I'm talking about. It's not the 'can't live without you' kind of emotion. The kind of love I mean is a positive, life affirming, connected energy.

We've already touched on the idea that we relate to each other on the nonverbal, or energetic, level. The interesting thing is that you choose this energy each day. You can either crawl out of bed (and drag yourself through the day) or you can choose to start each day with a connection to gratitude and love. By choosing the connection each day, you have the ability to project love everywhere you go and, in return, people respond.

Energy sounds like such a 'woo woo' concept, but we all read each other's energy every day. For example, if you sit at Starbucks watching people come in to get their morning coffee, I bet you can tell a lot about what kind of day they are having just by experiencing the energy they are projecting. Are they angry? Frustrated? Happy? Energetic? All these you will pick up on without ever saying a word to anyone. When you were a kid, you could tell what mood your mom was in instantly when you got home because this ability to read energy is engrained in our being.

We are especially sensitive to those we already have a deep emotional connection to. How many times has your spouse looked at you and asked, "What's going on? You aren't right somehow." Even if you thought you were hiding your emotions very well, you still give off energy that tells the truth and so they can still sense when things aren't right. We read this nonverbal energy all the time and it is often much more important than the words we use because we can, and do, lie. How often do you say you are fine when you aren't? Energy doesn't lie.

Once you grasp how much effect this nonverbal communication has on everyone you encounter, then you also realize how easily you can choose to project a positive emotion out into the world – and the most positive emotion is love.

Let's go back to the coffee shop. Let's say you are now standing in line waiting on coffee.

Did you notice how many people are avoiding eye contact and occupying themselves with distractions - all so they won't have to chat or make any sort of connection with anyone in the building, including the staff?

They are all projecting a self interested, closed energy and, as a result, everyone ignores everyone else. Yet, if just one person smiled, made eye contact and actually acknowledged the others in line, almost everyone responds in a positive fashion and suddenly the mood is entirely different.

This is how much control you have over your environment and how much control you have over how people respond to you. If you feel people aren't treating you well or that you keep having the same issues over and over in your life, then you must accept the responsibility and start right now giving love.

Don't confuse giving love with 'loving others' or loving what they do. This type of love isn't a shared emotion, nor does it have anything to do with deservedness. It's all about existing in the present and controlling your own energy. In order for you to receive love, peace and gratitude from others, you must send out these same emotions. You must try and help others experience Love, Peace, and Abundance. Remember that what we send out we attract back to us, so in order for your life to go from chaos to calm, you must take responsibility for the type of energy you give to others. In that way, you are also taking control of what you receive – which will be love. In this way love is very much like forgiveness. Forgiveness isn't about the person you forgive; it's about you and allowing yourself to release negative emotions and move forward.

Of course, the next question I usually get when we talk about love is that if our soul chooses this life and we can be connected to our inner self and give love, why are there so many hurt, angry and even criminal people?

Two words: we choose. Just as our spirit chose our current personality to experience this life in, the human part of us still chooses to connect with that spirit and grow or to shut it off and refuse to grow. People can allow themselves to become damaged by circumstances and events. Then they hold on to those emotions and relive them constantly. They have no idea that love is the cure, the release.

If you're co-creating this life, and you are, you're 100% responsible for what you experience.

You have to give what you want to experience in return, no matter the circumstances. For example, if you are in a tense and difficult work environment, you can choose to let go of the past, live in the now and each day start with the awareness that you can choose to give love. The interesting thing is that you don't directly change the people you deal with, but your view of them changes - that is the catalyst.

Each morning, as you sit and meditate to make your connection, think about those co-workers that are making your life difficult. Then, think of at least one thing about each co-worker you are grateful for. When you do this, your interaction with that person will change; not because they changed, but because you did. You can genuinely see something positive about them and, as you project that feeling, they will respond. In a very short period of time, you will be astonished at how well you are now working together in what seemed an impossible situation a few short months or weeks before.

Water Crystals

It may sound farfetched that the energy you project could have such an incredible effect, but it's true. After World War II, a Japanese scientist named Dr. Masaru Emoto, conducted many experiments to study the effect of ideas, words and music upon the molecules of water.

His groundbreaking research showed that the formation of water crystals is deeply affected by their environment. In one experiment, he took the same water divided into 3 Petri dishes and, focusing on the first one, he thought loving thoughts. With the 2nd, he thought hateful thoughts; with the 3rd, he ignored it completely. Then he froze the water and observed the crystal formation.

The 1st dish was perfect beautiful crystalline structure, the 2nd was ugly and distorted and the 3rd had really no structure at all. He drew the conclusion that if one crystal of water can be affected by external stimuli that are not physical, then we have a great deal of control over our world.

There is a story about a former prisoner of war that illustrates this. His captors thought that by giving him only a slice of bread and putrid water to drink, the prisoner would surely perish. So, each day, they offered only one piece of hard crusty bread and brown water that was near sludge.

Yet, each day the prisoner was healthy and not the least bit sick. This went on for some time and the guards were baffled. Anyone else who drank and ate that same regimen was literally dead within days, but week after week this one prisoner was alive and well. What they did not know was that each day the prisoner focused his love and gratitude on that nasty water. The water aligned with that energy and changed from something harmful to something that kept his body going.

We frequently project problems that may occur in the future and, thus, we bring them to pass. Have you ever dreaded a family gathering because you thought one or two people were going to cause a problem? How often was there a problem? Most of the time, I would guess. Yet, if you had taken control of your emotions, stayed in the present and entered that family gathering in a spirit of love, it probably would have had an entirely different outcome.

When you act out of love, you get some additional help in the form of guidance. It's not like a big finger comes out of the sky and points the way, but it's more an intuitive feeling. That intuition can be developed to a high level which allows you to discern the right path in many situations. If you want to be, and ask to be, guided you will receive that guidance. It's as if the clouds part and the path is clear where a moment before you were in complete confusion. We all need guidance, sometimes more than other times, but when it comes, we can mistakenly brush it aside if we aren't connected and aware.

I'm the first to admit that I can be stubborn when guidance shows itself. I've even been known to argue about highway directions with a voice that led me thousands of miles from home to have what was probably the most intense spiritual experience of my life. We all have that tendency sometimes because we allow our reason to get in the way.

When you think of things in a purely logical sense, gratitude and love are these soft cushy ideas that you might think shouldn't have a big effect on our lives as a whole – but they do.

We can easily get caught up in the thought process that we know probably 90% of the whats, wheres and whys of our world. But that's a fallacy. I would suggest it's more like 10% - if that. There is a lot we don't know, but we do get glimpses of things bigger than our understanding and love is one way that is revealed.

Love has a transformative and redeeming power that no one can really grasp until they experience or witness it. Think back to the example of Jesus or Gandhi. In the last minutes of life, they sent love and forgiveness to their murderers. Not only is it hard to grasp how they could do that with their dying breath, it is also hard to fathom the love their acts have generated through their followers.

There is a story that many people have heard of about Khamisa Azim. He experienced a parent's worst nightmare when his twenty-year-old son was murdered. Tariq was delivering pizza to an address and was shot by a fourteen-year-old gang member. Rather than get lost in the despair of his loss, Azim chose to give forgiveness and send love to his son's murderer.

He started a foundation in Tariq's honor to help break the cycle of youth violence by saving lives, teaching peace and planting seeds of hope. Azim even tried to get the governor of California to pardon the boy who killed his son.

One month after starting the foundation, Azim asked Ples Felix to join him. Ples was the grandfather and guardian of the young boy that killed Azim's son. Together, the two men have reached over 20 million people with their message of non-violence and forgiveness. This is just one example of how far love and forgiveness can take you, but there are many more out there.

Many people that you encounter every day have no idea how to give love because they have never received this type of love; the kind that is unconditional, pure and abundant.

If they have experienced any love at all, it most probably conditional, hurtful and brief. They become guarded and closed off and this dimenishes their ability to reconnect to their spirit – the self within the self. Introverted and fearful people can come across as withdrawn and some might think they have a better chance of connecting than some other people. But they aren't connected to their inner selves; they are just hiding from everyone else.

When you give only love – in a pure and unconditional way, you give off a tremendous energy. Other people feel this energy, whether they consciously realize it or not. For example, have you ever met a friend you were once close to after an absence of several years?

Are you astounded how you can pick that relationship up immediately as if they'd never been gone a day? That is because you are both giving off the same energy the two of you shared years earlier, so you immediately connect.

We all have the tendency to close ourselves off when we experience something negative. It can be something small, like avoiding a coworker because you were offended by something they said, or as large as choosing never to have a romantic relationship again because you have failed in the past. The reason doesn't matter; you consciously choose to disconnect from that aspect of your life and it sets up a roadblock to pure love. Over time, those little (and big) roadblocks add up and your heart becomes encrusted and weighed down.

The good news is that, just like you chose to allow those events and circumstances to weigh down your heart, you can choose to kick them off one by one.

I'm not suggesting that it happens overnight or that some universal spirit will force you to have a breakdown and drive to Santa Fe, but it might! Odds are, you will be somewhere in-between and just as I was a complete newbie to the full depth of these ideas when I went to Santa Fe, over time, I have worked on myself and peeled back the onion of my heart. Now I understand the importance of projecting the energy of love in everything I do.

Am I perfect at it? No, but that in itself is perfect because it reminds me I still have a lot of spiritual growth on the horizon. But the only way I'm going to make progress on that spiritual journey is to reconnect as often as possible to my spirit and align myself with loving thoughts, then watch what happens.

The Bible even alludes to this order of growth with the passage that starts, "Seek ye first the kingdom of God."

This passage instructs us to connect to the power first and

foremost; only then will our desires manifest. Funny thing about that though, your desires change.

Wield Your Power Carefully

Have you ever been around someone who has just experienced his or her first taste of real power? Maybe it was a manager at your job that was promoted and then proceeded to run off just about everyone there. It's almost like they have a magic wand and no idea how to control the thing. Before you know it, they've turned everyone into toads! I wasn't much different before I had my experience in Santa Fe.

I had a little glimpse of the power that exists within each of us and how you can create your own life. So I thought, "Hey I want more and better stuff – that would be a great life!" I figured that I would achieve that by making money and having a successful business and that's what happened. I created this wealth, but somehow it got out of control, like a wayward magic wand. I was unhappy, losing power, losing strength and when I ultimately said that I would go anywhere and do anything - that I wanted to know what the answer to life really is, only then did I surrender and allow my heart to fully open to the experience. Instantly, I was full of energy and power. I gained an unbelievable amount of insight and wisdom in that short two week span.

It opened my eyes to many of the lessons that I needed to experience. I went with the question, "What is the essence of life?" Now I know – it's love. I experienced many lessons and truths on that trip. For example, my experience at Satsang taught me to connect; to listen within myself and to be still. I also learned from my friend turning down my invitation to come and photograph my experience. I still believed it would take place somehow and, within an hour, I'd met and connected with a world-class local photographer.

The power of belief can bring things into being even if you have no idea how it's going to happen.

The stop in Colorado Springs taught me that we are all guided. If you want to be guided, you will be.

In all those experiences, I became more aware and once you tap into awareness, it is like a floodgate because the awareness escalates. If you choose to surrender, any ordinary person (no matter their past or circumstances) can be redeemed, forgiven and then can reconnect to that perfect spirit – the self within the self.

You can choose how you use your awareness and power, but if you only sporadically or partially connect to that true loving awareness, you will not ever be fully happy. That's not to say you will hate your life. There are many people that I would say are very 'good' people. They work hard, go to church and spend time with their families. But they often feel this little nagging in their soul that there is something more for them. They are feeling that intuitive knowledge that their spirit needs challenge and growth. Some choose to take that challenge and open themselves to a new loving journey. Others don't.

The most frustrating thing is to gain great wisdom and knowledge, but then over time to lose that connection. I know. It happened to me. Oh, it took a while after I returned from Santa Fe – a few years in fact – but, eventually, that connection waned. I wasn't at full strength yet, so to speak, and life crept back in as it often does. But the awesome thing about the awareness that you can give love is that once you open the door, you can't shut it. Eventually, you will have to walk through it fully.

There are many people on this earth who are convinced that emotion is bad and that showing emotion is even worse. Over time, people with this belief system can build tremendous walls. They don't want to feel because it's hard to work through those emotions.

They avoid feeling anything and cut off their emotions completely.

When you are growing your awareness and tapping into the power that love has to transform you and those around you, it can be natural to pull back from that at first. It's hard to allow yourself to really feel – especially in front of others. What if I break down? Will they think I'm weak? Or that I've lost it? Or that I'm having a mid-life crisis??

All these 'what ifs' race through your head while you think of something, anything, to help stay in control of your emotions. I'm not sure who first created this belief system that we are supposed to hide emotions, but I know it does a lot of damage. We are emotional beings, all of us, even the men and we need that emotional release to allow our energy to flow freely. Now, I'm not saying that you must always keep a wad of tissues in your pocket because you've suddenly become Niagara Falls, but you should not have to reject emotions in order to exist!

You were created a perfect being and your emotions exist to help expand your awareness and love for yourself and others. You learn to harness those emotions to work for you, rather than just rejecting them. By allowing yourself to fully feel emotions, you provide the foundation for feeling pure and honest love.

So many people have spent literally years hiding from old hurts or trauma that when they start to work through and release that pain, it hurts. But it is important to understand that it is only painful for a short time and then you can release the hurt and let go. Some find it incredulous that people who have suffered greatly can then turn around and forgive the source of that pain and express love toward them, just like the example of Azim. I can't imagine having to experience that, but I do know that love is the response.

Chapter 9

Living Present

I've shared a lot of information so far and some of these ideas are probably completely new to you, but you don't have to know all the answers to make positive strides in your life. There will not be a quiz at the end, so stop worrying about being 'right' all the time! Moving forward is not just about making more money or accomplishing big goals. You can do those things too, but the real forward motion comes from searching inside yourself for your own version of peace and happiness.

I don't have all the answers – in fact, the more I learn, the more I realize that our human minds can only comprehend so much (and even, then we understand imperfectly). But that's okay. You don't have to know how the wind blows to enjoy the breeze and so it is with the ideas of universal consciousness and soul reincarnation. You don't have to understand them or believe the way I do, but you must seek out your own personal connection to the power hidden within yourself.

This power is hidden because we pile on all the hurt, regret and past events right on top of it. We feel stressed and hurried like our lives are a perpetual treadmill. I felt this way even after I'd had the tremendous spiritual awakening that was my Santa Fe experience. It would have been really easy to beat myself up and say, "Well if you really had such a great experience, then why did you let it go?" But that was not the lesson I was supposed to learn. The real lesson is the fact that this illusion of life and the chaos we encounter every day will always be there and you can't pretend it doesn't exist, or that it doesn't affect you, because it's just not true. This may all be an illusion, but doesn't invalidate the experience.

We all have trials and tribulations, both large and small, that we must deal with and sometimes our responses aren't as good as we might like them to be. I'm no exception. But I know there is a peaceful existence to strive for and that makes me want it all the more.

I was shown a partial and brief view of this perfection in Santa Fe, but I wasn't ready yet to really grasp all the implications it held. It took me 16 years of studying and learning (and getting it wrong a lot of times!) to reach this point, and I'm still learning. All we can do is manage today - right now. There is only now and you are creating your future and your past from this moment. There is only now, past and future are being created from the now constantly.

One of the biggest obstacles anyone encounters in uncovering their true self is holding on to the past. This does not necessarily mean focusing on a negative past event; sometimes positive events create just as big an obstacle. For example, have you ever been around a middle aged person who constantly talks about the 'glory days', maybe their high school or college years? Annoying, isn't it? It annoys us because we can clearly see that they are giving up all that they could be experiencing right now to hang on to something that can do nothing for them. They are hiding from their fear, anger and even disappointment as to how life has turned out and it feels better to escape into that memory of a time when they felt happy. But it is an illusion and one that really stagnates growth.

Of course, negative past events can have a much stronger effect. We each choose to hold on to anger and hurt, replaying the events repeatedly (even years later) and savoring those terrible emotions. Life is too short to give control of your future and today's possibilities to a person or event that happened years ago. Everything is manifested through your thoughts, so when you hold on to a negative thought you are condemning yourself to have more bad experiences. It is a learned skill to choose to release anger quickly, but I can say with confidence that one skill has allowed more growth in my personal life than anything else. I don't experience extended anger about anything and that keeps things from escalating and creating discomfort for not only me, but also for my family, friends, co-workers and strangers that I encounter during the course of my day.

Don't get me wrong; I'm not a saint and there are times I feel that hot emotion flare up like a tropical sun. But I've taught myself to recognize it for what it really is, an illusion, and let it go. This isn't about the absence of emotion; we all have emotions. It is about recognizing them and responding positively.

I talk a great deal about living in the present and that is also a learned skill. At first, it sounds easy to think that you can just deal with what is in front of you. Don't worry about the future or the past; just deal with today. In reality, this is pretty challenging. All our lives, we have been taught to worry about the future and constantly go over the 'what-if' scenarios in our minds for each situation. But there is only one outcome, so basically you are wasting 90% of your time and energy trying to guess an outcome, rather than spending 100% of your time experiencing right now. That is how I got to be a millionaire who felt like he'd wasted his whole life. I had spent all my time striving for this 'future' and had to learn what it meant to fully be connected and present every minute.

You have to teach yourself to control your thoughts. In order to do that, you must become aware of your thoughts. Again, this takes some practice. Think about sitting at your desk at work. How much of what you do is focused on the past or on the future? Are you compiling reports about what happened last month or putting together proposals for what will happen next month? Odds are, you are doing some of both. Because we spend so much of our time thinking this way, we naturally transfer the same thoughts and actions to our personal lives.

Maybe you are still thinking about the stunt the kids pulled yesterday while also trying to figure out how to pay for next year's family vacation. Your mind is completely disconnected from what is happening right now. How often do you see the first leaves of fall and think, "Where did summer go?" It feels like you missed it and the sad thing is, you did.

The answer of course is connection: the connection to

you. Even if it's just a few minutes at the start of your day, that connection brings you right to the present. It heightens your awareness and pulls you into that space in which you are thinking and acting on purpose rather than reacting to the chaos of life.

Sometimes I sit outside at my home in Florida and watch the sunset. There are few things more renewing and invigorating than a pure, beautiful sunset. It feels like a welling up of possibility and peace. I can think about those ideas and concepts that are beyond my 'to-do' list and it reminds me, not only of what is important, but of what isn't. This allows me to re-prioritize and resist the tendency to allow urgent things to crowd out the important ones.

I anticipate that you will learn faster than I did, but there is one thing I know for certain: we are all on our own journey and no two paths are ever the same. Making these changes in your life often involves disruptive changes in relationships and careers.

Feeling responsible for those disruptions is something you must release. You are not responsible for anyone else's journey but your own. You being the healthiest and most centered, connected version of yourself is the biggest gift you can give those in your life, even if they don't understand it at first. Sometimes that means you have to remove yourself from a relationship or situation for your own growth. But realize that it is for their growth as well.

Maintaining the status quo is the easy thing to do, but often it is also the most destructive because those who are maintaining are also dying a slow death. They are denying the need for their personal growth because they are not connecting with their true self.

I knew years ago that I had to present this message, yet I chose to maintain my own status quo. I wasn't horribly unhappy, but there was this nagging that tugged at my soul because I knew there was more. The longer I denied that feeling, the more I felt I was just killing time and not really accomplishing what I was here for.

The reason I'm at peace now is because I'm actually stepping outside of my comfort zone, doing something that is a little scary. I can say it has disrupted my life tremendously, but for the first time, I can honestly say I'm at peace with that. Now that I'm doing what I feel like I'm supposed to be doing, it feels like peace. Is it total peace right now? No, I'm a human being. I'm not Jesus Christ and I'm not Buddha. This is still my journey and I don't want anyone to think I'm in perfect harmony all the time, every hour, every minute of every waking moment.

My level of harmony is exponentially greater now than it was before and it's growing daily because I'm actually working on it and fostering it.

I think it is the fear of disruption that keeps people unhappy. They want to go along with the status quo and they tell themselves, "Hey, this is how it's been. Maybe I'm just supposed to be unhappy." So they start looking for ways to fill that void without actually addressing the problem. That's where you get into the alcoholism, addiction, the girlfriend on the side, even the mid-life crisis type behavior. It's because they're not looking for their personal spiritual connectedness where they should be. All they know is that they feel the void and keep trying to fill it up with something.

Writing this book has done tremendous things for me. By that, I mean it has pushed my own growth forward. I committed to write it with the knowledge that it may never be published and people might never read it. Once I accepted that and was okay with it, the words poured out.

I couldn't hold on to that illusion of what the future might hold for this message; I just had to write that message down.

That is my journey. It is not about getting credit, notice as an author or experiencing the change that people experience because of what I've written. My journey was just to write it. Of course, I do hope it helps someone. Even if, however, I never know of that, I know I will have accomplished what I'm here for. When you live your purpose, it gives you the freedom to live with reckless abandon. To understand that what you experience right now, today, is of paramount importance.

My own growth occurs when I push myself and that is true for most people, I think. You have to seek out the answers and choose to educate yourself.

There's no replacement for a curious mind. It's easy to sit in front of the television each night and zone out. It's an escape, a panacea for what we really want. But to get to a better place, it takes work and consistent effort.

I can't motivate you to make that effort; only you can do it. Sadly, you also can't motivate someone else to experience something they may not be ready for. Also, if you are growing and they are not, at some point it may cause a rift in the relationship.

Some also use this as an excuse not to grow. They don't want their relationships to change, so they slide into denial. But eventually it catches up with you.

Change is inevitable, no matter how hard you try to keep things the same. Your only choice is to grow; otherwise you are stepping backward. Sometimes I think about why I didn't write this book when I was first told to.

Sure there was some denial, but I also think I wasn't ready. I wasn't at the place in my own growth where I was ready to share my own experience. I'm not perfect by any stretch of the imagination and I've made a lifetime of mistakes. Those mistakes have brought me here to share my knowledge with you. I was a completely different person at the age of 35 than I am now at the age of 51 and I'm sure I will be even more different at the age of 65 than I am now. The difference is that, now, I embrace and welcome that change with open arms.

You have to keep yourself grounded and be yourself. You're here now; experience it to the greatest of your ability. Do it with all the love and reckless abandon you can. Savor it. It's okay if you don't have the answer to every question. Just go back to making it simple because complexity can make it overwhelming. We struggle so much as humans to comprehend incomprehensible concepts and, in doing so, those concepts become imperfect. It's like trying to fit God into the image that he's the old guy with gray hair and gray beard who lives in the sky.

By trying to understand the concept of the universe or what we think of as God, we fit it into a box in our struggle to comprehend it. In truth, we can ever only comprehend it by becoming one with it. But even if we can't have that complete oneness, that doesn't mean we shouldn't strive to understand the incomprehensible, loving energy that is us.

It really is simple. Connect, be aware and choose. Choose only love; give only love. That's it. Just by doing those simple things, you can progress father in your spiritual growth in a year than you may have your entire life thus far. It was never intended to be hard; it's just different than what we are used to. You can use these ideas to create a peaceful, less stressful existence, but you can also use them as tools to survive very difficult circumstances.

No matter who you are, you will experience tough times. They may be financial, interpersonal or even physical. People who are close to you will pass away. You will experience trauma within various relationships.

You may even know someone who has an illness or contract a difficult and devastating illness yourself, but that doesn't mean you can't or won't be happy.

Remember how we talked about the fact that you see news reports of children in Third World countries playing in garbage heaps? They don't know they aren't supposed to be happy. They just live in the moment and accept what happiness they can have right now. There is no sadness for what they don't have because they aren't aware they should be sad.

When you experience something very physically or emotionally trying, the typical (and often first) reaction is sadness over the loss. But, in this case, the loss is over the possibility of the future, not the reality of it. Let me give you an example. If a dear loved one passes away, you experience sadness and regret. Of course, you know they are now at peace and in a wonderful existence, but you still long for your own experience of having them in your life.

You imagine all the holidays without that person and family gatherings they will now be absent from. It's okay to be sad because here again; this is not about the absence of emotion, it is just understanding that to cling to or galvanize that emotion of sadness is what is damaging. Feel it, understand it, love it and release it. Do what Dr. Hew Len says to do to with all your memories: say, "I am sorry. Please forgive me. I love you. Thank you."

This is an example of living in the future. We are focused on what we will miss in the future because a particular person is gone. Now you know that this isn't the path to happiness and by teaching yourself to live in the present, when a difficult situation such as a death occurs you are able to celebrate their life without focusing on your own perception of loss. Getting past difficult experiences is all about taking life one day at a time.

Let yesterday and all its tears go. Don't focus on a future that isn't here yet. Instead, focus on today; focus on now and what you can do to find your peace and happiness.

This is the same idea that many 12-step programs use and there is a reason for that. Focusing on now releases us from expectations about tomorrow or regrets about the past and allows us to direct our energy to what we need to experience. This makes us much stronger individuals and gives us the courage and confidence to proceed.

As humans, we are a co-dependent bunch. So much of our lives are spent trying to 'fix' someone else. Perhaps it is a family member, spouse or friend, but we often focus on their issues and how we can make them better, to our own detriment. It can be very difficult to realize that sometimes you have to let go.

No one wants to let go of something they have spent part of their lives putting energy and focus on. It is painful, not to mention disruptive, in many ways. But at some point, we must have the strength to allow that person to travel his or her own path.

You can think of it like raising a child. They have to stumble and fall in order to learn and grow – then, eventually, you have to release them and allow them to go their own way.

We also have to protect ourselves from those well meaning individuals who are trying to 'fix' us! As you can imagine, my beliefs are not all that popular with some of the people in my life, but they work for me. I know how they feel because I feel the same way about some of their beliefs! But I have to connect with what works for me and, as I grow as a person, they will come to see that.

There will never be a deliriously happy existence with everyone I know simply because we are all different. It's not about making others the same as me. It's about me giving them all the love I can and allowing them to be them.

No matter how much you disagree with someone, giving love is the answer. You can disagree on virtually everything else, but love is love and it can't be denied. Everyone feels it; everyone wants more of it and you have it to give. The changes that you make in your life will sometimes draw negative attention that makes you want to crawl under a rock!

By responding with love instead of dread or fear, you diffuse those negative emotions. Any situation in which you don't know what to do, love is the answer. People feel your genuine sincerity and warmth and it is immediately noticeable.

The world we live in today is cynical and jaded to the point that just to encounter someone with a smile on their face is rare and someone emanating love is about as common as a white alligator! But you have to remember that you create 100% of your experience. If you focus on the cynical and jaded attitudes that are so prevalent, or the negative events going on in the world, then that is what you will perceive life to be. However, if you focus on love, then that will create and permeate your experience. It is all about being responsible for your own experience.

Love makes you a beacon of calm in a sea of despair. I remember what it was like to worry or lie awake at night, letting my anger boil over.

I never want to feel the full depth of those emotions again. I have the ability to use my own awareness to head off that negativity and it gives me confidence to keep going. It will keep you going, too.

Chapter 10

Two Questions

All of the ideas and experiences I have written in this book were the result of asking two questions:

What is life about?

Why am I here?

Each of these questions contains just four short words, but the universe and all existence are contained in their answers. Remember the quote that small minds talk about people, average minds talk about events and great minds talk about ideas.? That has really been the progression of my own journey.

I started out with me as the focus, the center of my universe. All I held onto was what I could understand at the moment. I couldn't see much beyond the work I did that day or education I received that week as to what my life might be like five years or even one year down the road.

Over time, I thought that to grow I had to focus on making things happen. So, I went to work trying to figure out a way to become financially secure. I did this because I thought if I had money, I would be happy and that it would allow me to have endless choices. I had no idea in the beginning that money and happiness weren't connected to each other at all.

Finally, I realized that the large ideas of connectedness, universal consciousness and the illusion we live everyday were the ideas that I needed to figure out for myself. I finally understood that embracing the quest to solve the equation of life for answers was the real pursuit. The rest was just noise.

As you have figured out by reading the previous chapters, understanding what life is all about didn't happen for me overnight – in fact, it is still happening because it is a continual journey. I know I may not ever really understand all of it, but that doesn't mean I won't try . It is so important to understand that your soul exists and has always existed.

You are bigger than this life and you are part of the universal consciousness that never dies.

The idea that my soul chose to be here and that I could use this life to align myself as closely as possible with a pure and abiding love was the starting point; a catalyst in my personal growth in many ways. In reality, though, it was just the starting point. Up until then, I'd just been treading water and floundering around trying to figure out my life. I was tossed this way and that by circumstance, but now I know circumstances don't matter. Your emotional state of being matters and if you can control your thoughts every second, then you can control your circumstances.

So what is life about? The answer to that question is different for everyone, yet the same. I know I sound like a slick $500per hour lawyer but the statement is true. We are all here to learn how to connect to our inner selves and to move ever closer to that perfect connection. But it will be a very different journey for you than it has been for me because we are each different souls on our own journeys.

Still, even though we have seemingly vast differences sometimes, the meaning of life for all of us is about connecting. That's it. It's not about how many cars you have or where you vacationed last summer. Again, that's just noise.

It's not about obeying a grey-haired man in the sky or burning incense to the right deity either. Life is about the discovery of self, of who you really are and how you can change your behaviors to be more in alignment with that true self.

When you are in this incarnation, it is all about alignment with purpose. For example, say you are supposed to be a singer, but all you think about are the obstacles. How far do you think you would get?

A few years back, the world was introduced to Susan Boyle, an incredible singer. She was a somewhat homely 47-year-old woman from England and she shocked the world with her performances. She proved that it's never too late to align with your purpose and there is always a way if you focus on what you can do instead of what you can't.

It is interesting to contemplate that we, as souls, are all here for the same purpose and that is to grow. Yet, we each have our own distinct goals and objectives. We are each here to experience this existence as deeply as possible and yet each of us has individual character points to refine.

Each of our souls planned this journey before we were born, but within that framework there is a lot of room for free will, so we each choose whether or not to accept the experience as it was originally laid out. Often, the actual experience of living is that the effect of certain experiences and events is so much larger and more complex than we ever imaged that it takes us in a completely different direction. That is what this life is.

You have chosen to live this life and you know you have all the power. But when you are born, it's almost like a little amnesia sets in and we have to discover our souls once again. We are predestined insomuch as we are intended to experience certain ideas and our souls chose those things beforehand. But the real beauty is our ability to adjust the dream and our path as we encounter the complexity of life - and this fosters spiritual growth.

While your mind might not remember the plan that you created as a soul before you were born, your inner self (your soul) does remember. In fact, one of the functions of your inner self is that it provides hunches or feelings that we must each follow in order to gain access to all we were meant to be. Those ideas or hunches, when acted upon, allow you to explore this life's potential to the fullest.

There is a feeling and innate knowing when you come into contact with your life's purpose. I talk all the time about the 'truth tingle,' that emotion or tingle that I get when something really connects.

It is a surge of energy that I feel and know that certain thing is right. Many people experience this same energy surge. You just know this is where you are supposed to be and what you are supposed to be doing. This feeling is your soul giving you hints as to your direction, but you still have free will.

You can still choose to follow those urges or not.

It can seem like I'm talking in a circle and, in a way, that is the correct image. Life is all about getting back to that perfect place of soul connection again and moving forward in your growth. Your soul starts in a perfect place, but then chooses to have more life experiences to exist within that space even more perfectly than before. That is the meaning of life. Connecting, experiencing, growing and changing. You are born, live, die and do it all again, each time, changing a little more.

It was interesting for me that once the realization dawned on me that the meaning of life had nothing to do with my daily worries and was all about not getting caught in the illusion of this life, many things became really insignificant that had once been important.

Once you have a shift in perception like that, you realize that money, status, career and things like appearances are all distractions from the real reason you are here.

I am here to connect with myself (and even with other people) on an emotional, soulful level - not the superficial level. So, I find I have less patience for that kind of thing. I'm not making any judgments because we are all on our own path. I am just moving along on my journey and it doesn't include those superficial trappings anymore.

When you're grateful and thankful for your life, thankful for everything, and you exist in the present with a positive loving attitude, giving and sending love, then you are able to make progress.

Life is about getting back into alignment and if you think of life on a scale of 0 to 100 (with 100 being perfect alignment), you may be at 40 on the alignment scale. But then, by giving love, you accelerate and start to go in a positive direction. You have to remember that you are always going toward power or away from power – there is no such thing as the status quo.

When you think about life from this perspective, does it even make sense that you would hold on to anger or hurt from events in the past? Events that didn't really matter anyway? Love, love, love is the cure. You need to be able to forgive yourself and others because forgiveness gets rid of past karma and attachment. This frees you to progress further and be closer to this power. But if you get stuck and fall back into giving anger, doubt or fear, this pushes you away from that connection to the self within the self.

I realize these are big ideas, but it really is that simple. If you give anything other than a positive emotion such as joy, bliss and love, then you are drifting away from that source of power and growth. You know it and feel it when it happens.

First, it is the stress of holding in the negative emotions and then it manifests itself physically with headaches, muscles aches and even heartburn. This is when we end up popping antacids like they are candy in an attempt to cover it up.

But the outside world isn't creating this experience; we are. We are choosing to hold on to those negative emotions, irritations and hurts. We only hurt ourselves. We can also choose to release the negative. We can lance it off like an old puss-filled boil and, once it's gone, we feel sweet relief.

We are not meant to live in chaos and turmoil; we are meant to live in peace and harmony. I don't mean the kind of 'world peace' that beauty queens pretend to promote, but the kind of peace that happens with your inner self when you have connected and are in harmony with your purpose. Of course if we all did that, there might really be world peace, but that's another book!

You can choose to progress and you can also resist, but you are in control of that decision. I knew I was supposed to deliver a message, but then resisted and didn't do it for years. The great thing is that, no matter what you are resisting right now, you can change your mind and reconnect just like I did. Now, I'm writing this book in order to deliver that message I was always supposed to get across. That is what I believe my purpose for this life to be and that is why I am here.

Now, I have no idea what the message will accomplish once it's released, but the sharing of it was for the growth of my own soul and it has already accomplished that, so it doesn't matter what the ultimate outcome will be because I have done the part I was supposed to finish and now it's out of my hands.

Who knows? It may influence someone to change their life and connect to their own reason for being in this life. But I may never know, and that's okay. I do know that we are all pebbles in a pond and every action we take influences the lives and journeys of others in unimaginable ways.

As I'm writing this chapter, we are moving into the holiday season and one of the movies that most people watch every year is "It's a Wonderful Life." I especially like the old black and white version with Jimmy Stewart. This movie shows the powerful interconnectedness we all have and how we influence the lives of others in either a positive or negative way just by existing.

It also shows the power of love and gratitude. Needless to say, my Spidey truth tingle goes on full alert because it is a powerful reminder that if we give only love, that is exactly what will be returned to us and that is our true wealth.

The complexity of life is overwhelming and we don't have to have everything figured out in a neat little package. You don't have to know what tomorrow will bring because you are creating your tomorrow today. You can just accept that giving love is the key and start on your own journey of self discovery.

You don't have to know why Pluto is no longer a planet or if there are bug-eyed aliens on the other side of the Milky Way. You just have to want to figure out you. The thoughts you had yesterday created your experience today and today's thoughts will create tomorrow. This means you can choose at noon, or 8:00 pm, or whatever time, on any given day to change something in your life. That might be something as small as slipping a note in your kids' lunchbox telling them how wonderful they are or it may be as big as changing careers, but you are creating something new no matter the action.

The ultimate truth, the ultimate reality, is the alignment with the self within the self and you get there by love and forgiveness. Seeing the alignment and believing you can make it is all it takes. If you want to pray, pray. Many people call on that Christ Consciousness to help them make decisions and gain that connection. You are calling on the universal power all of our souls were, and are, a part of and asking for guidance. It will arrive in the form of urges or your own 'truth tingle.' Maybe a voice will even come that lets you know when you've come across the right path.

Just like there is more than one way up a mountain, there are many paths to connection so don't limit yourself or allow old belief systems to inhibit your experience in this life. There are always obstacles and challenges to overcome.

Just because you are following a path toward joy and peace, others in your life may not be and this will inevitably cause conflict. Those ordeals exist to challenge your soul, as anyone who has ever raised a teenager can attest to! But even those trying times occur for your growth as a person and, by giving love, you can weather the storm without being dragged down into the muck.

There are many people who are struggling with their lives. They feel trapped by old belief systems, by guilt. They feel they can't make a big life change without having first rescued every person around them.

Our relationships are extremely complex and they flex and change over time, but that doesn't decrease their complexity. When you fully understand the idea that what you send out is returned and that you create your reality, the next obvious realization is that you must take responsibility for the chaos you experience.

It may feel like it's not your fault, but how you react to circumstance is your responsibility and don't for one second think you didn't bring it on in the first place. You know how, when you were a kid, and saw a fight on the playground, the one who instigated the fight wasn't the one who got sent to the principal's office? It was the one who hit back who got into trouble, even if he was just defending himself.

But that person also attracted the attention of the bully in the first place. So, no one is really innocent. Don't lie to yourself or convince yourself that you are guiltless - you're not. Take responsibility.

Think about that person at the office who you don't like. How much time do you spend dreading running into them? When you finally do, it always goes pretty much how you expect – badly. But the thing is, if you think it will be bad, it will.

What if, instead, you actively chose to give only love? I'm not talking about striking up an office romance, but I do mean that you focus on those positive qualities that person has and, instead of dreading being in their presence, you stay in the present and give love. It can and will change the dynamic immediately, yet the only person that changed was you. So it makes sense that the real obstacle to a positive experience before was YOU! Annoying, isn't it? If you can fix it, then you broke it. Just take it as the truth it is.

I plan to spend my life being open to new ideas and new experiences. The more open I am, the more interesting and soul satisfying things come into my life. I guess I'm kind of like the guy who is afraid to swim but then once he jumps into the deep end of the pool and experiences that joy, he's out scuba diving with the Great Whites. I want to go deep, to really seek that depth of understanding about who I am and what I am here for.

As humans, we love our ruts. In fact, we love them so much we'd rather keep doing what we've always done (even though it may be completely crappy) than try something new. We are an entire species of 'rutters' and we even teach our offspring not to aim too high or hope for too much. It's sad to see so many people like this when I know they can have so much more, experience so much more and be so much more of the person they were meant to be.

This message is one I want my family and friends to understand. I'm not a soapbox preacher or orator, but by writing this down I hope that they come to understand not only me, but themselves as well. They may feel like I'm trying to get them to understand, but I'm really trying to understand myself. I'm revealing myself, not influencing anyone else. Yet, if someone else can read my story and find something that helps them, then that is great too. I'm as imperfect as they come and if I can find more peace and joy in this life, so can they.

It's not about being dissatisfied with life right now, it's knowing there is so much more waiting for you to just tap in to.

Because so many people were raised with a heaping load of guilt as children, I get asked all the time if living to discover your true self isn't selfish. I can honestly say that living for you is the most selfish thing and most unselfish thing you can do at the same time. You can't really be as functional or offer as much to others in your life if you don't work on you first. You have to love unconditionally, and love yourself unconditionally, before you can ever give that love to someone else.

You have the power to create your life, but how can you do that if you convince yourself that it is somehow nobler to live for someone else and play the martyr? Each person has to listen to and follow their own heart; you can't do it for them. What exactly are you accomplishing by sacrificing yourself? You aren't helping their spirit grow. In fact, you are getting in the way!

You should be able to do anything you can do to make your own connection. That doesn't mean society will always agree with you. Still, you don't have to compromise. Just like we are a species of 'rutters,' we are also great compromisers. That's how I lost the progress I'd made in Santa Fe.

I comprised my way right back into my rut of comfort and old way of being, but not anymore. Now, I don't compromise. If that creates pain and suffering, it only creates pain and suffering if I perceive it as such. Just because someone doesn't like something doesn't mean it isn't the best thing. It may take days, weeks, years or even a lifetime for them to realize it, but that isn't your concern. You just have to stick to your own path.

You know, the greatest aspect of dealing with pain and suffering is that you realize your own alignment. It's a reminder that you have farther to go.

It points out the specific areas you still need to work on and, in that way, you can look at pain and suffering as a gift. It moves you further along the path than you might have traveled if it didn't exist. Celebrate the fact that you have pain and suffering in your life and that the way to get past it is to give love and offer forgiveness. It sounds so simple, but it's so profound.

If we go back to the scene of Christ's final hours, ask yourself how many people you know that could be nailed to a cross, look down and say, "Please forgive them, they know not what they do?" Could you do that? Would you? Would you be able to look down and forgive them knowing they were ending your life? I think most people would scream for their lawyer and threaten to haunt them forever. Yet, this is an example of someone so perfectly aligned and connected to that true source of power that he still had the presence of mind to give love and to forgive.

When Gandhi was assassinated, his last act was to clasp his hands and to forgive the person who killed him. It was so profound. You'd think he would have shock, anger or dismay on his face, but all he did was forgive the person who killed him. I just can't imagine it. Well, I can, but I'm not so sure I'd be able to respond in a similar manner. Yet, like I said, I'm still on my journey, so maybe I will get to that point one day.

If nothing else, I hope this book has dusted off some of the cobwebs in your mind and made you think about ideas that are bigger and more far reaching than you've ever thought about before. I also hope that it has driven home the idea that changing for the better starts by looking within and it is that journey that is the hardest.

I wish you joy, peace and, most of all, love.

My Cleansing Prayer

My healing process starts with the first step.

Lord please give me the strength to choose only love, the courage to give only love and the wisdom to realize I am human and shall make mistakes from time to time.

I thank you for allowing me this life opportunity and only hope that when my time on this earth is over, I will look back with no regrets. I will have no regrets of wasted time, lost opportunities, or about people that I have caused any pain or suffering.

As I write each passing line, I can feel a cleansing of my soul.

It is as if I am sifting through garbage, trying to find my inner self at the bottom. I realize now, more than ever, that I cannot stop until there is no more garbage.

For I know what will be left will be only love; the only real and absolute truth of life.

(Written by Joe Nealon on April 21st, 1995, to ease my pain)

I Believe

In these pages, I have shared a lot of stories, things I have experienced, have discovered, and continue to discover, on my life journey. That's all great, but what is the bottom line? I'm a bottom line kind of guy and after having traveled this path I'm on for over five decades now, I needed to write in plain and simple language what I believe. These 'laws' are not mine, I first encountered them in the teaching of Bashar and they have shapped my life ever since.

Here goes:

I believe that there are four universal laws:

1. You exist; you always have and you always will (you being your soul). You never die.

2. You are part of the One (universal power); it is you, you are it.

3. What you put out is what you get back.

4. Change is the only constant (except with regards to the first 3 laws).

As we exist and make our way through every day in this human experience, the only law that you have to look at is law number three. You create your life each day and the amount of effort you put into making that life great is up to you.

I believe that souls are born from the source of infinite power (this is why we are created in the image of God, because we are a piece of God made manifest). It is as if the universe is a vast ocean – we are all the same, yet each of us exists separately as well. Our existence is our gift from the universe and what we do with this life is our gift back to the universe.

Unlike babies, who need to be taught certain things when they are born, we already know everything we need to know; we just have to remember it. This is where earth comes in.

Earth is just one of an infinite number of places where you have experiences.

You choose to come to this realm to experience, which is another way to create. When you are done creating here, your soul will move on to the perfect place at the perfect time to create something new. In order for the universal power to truly know itself, it created you to have experiences that were different from itself in order to know itself as divine. God is Love. The opposite of love is fear. Therefore, if you experience anything other than love, it is not who you are.

Like all people, some souls progress faster, are at different levels, have different abilities and will learn different lessons. This is not the only reason we should be tolerant with each other, but it is a good one.

Imagine a five-year-old learning to count and then suddenly being put up against a math scholar from MIT. It is not really a fair comparison and we aren't here to compare our experience to anyone else's. We are each on our own path; it's not a better path or a worse one, just different.

We choose the life we are going to have before we arrive and what lesson that life will carry.

It might be overcoming anger, jealousy, greed or lust in order to learn unconditional love, forgiveness or compassion (and/or many other higher level concepts).

We do this in soul groups, so chances are that the people in your life have been with you in past lives before.

The soul of the person whom you now know as your wife may have been a brother, an aunt, a sister, an uncle, or a son in a previous existence.

Now, let's look at the 3rd law a little more in-depth: "What you put out is what you get back." Our thoughts, words and actions are what we use to co-create with the universal power. Therefore, your thoughts become beliefs and these are what you will manifest in your life.

This is why it is so important to guard against thoughts or ideas you do not want and replace them with thoughts of the life you would like to lead. Learn to follow your highest joy.

Here is where sages, gurus and mystical teachers come in and create some confusion. They say that to be one with the universal power is to have the absence of thoughts, to go to ground zero if you will, and not to be attached to anyone or anything.

This allows the individual to connect directly with the universal power. Self-help teachers today state that to get what you want, you simply think of your life the way that you want to it become. I am here to say, their ideas don't necessarily conflict with closely held beliefs you may already have; you can believe both.

Jesus said, "Seek ye first the kingdom of God." The translation of this idea is to go within and connect directly with the universal or 'God' power.

Then, allow this power to guide you, to work through you so that you may live your life in a divinely inspired way.

You can choose to picture the life you wish to live or not - it is your choice. We each have free will and you can make your life easier or harder.

Simply be you with all your heart and with all the love that you can give. It is that simple! Relax! You live forever, are universally powerful and are in control.

To be in total control, you have to give up control to the universal power (God) and have faith that what happens will be perfect.

To be in control or not to be in control, that's the question. Only you have the answer to.

This book is my answer to the question, "What is life about?" You have the answer to why you chose your life; now go find your purpose. Why, then, does it matter what we do in this life if we never die, live forever and are just here to experience living so that God can know itself experientially?

We live during a time of rapid change and if the world is to survive, we need to learn to live together with each other and with the planet or our world will cease to exist. We can't keep doing things the same way, so we have to change. My message is simple - love.

Love yourself, your neighbor, love the planet. Thoughts are things; love is the most powerful force in the universe. Use the lens of love to view the world as you would want it to be, not as it exists today.

All you need is love...
Love is all you really need

John Lennon

About the Author

Joe Nealon graduated from Sheridan College in 1982 with a business diploma. After graduation he worked a few jobs to get enough money to travel the world. Upon his return in 1983 he started to study the power of the mind by taking the Bob Proctor seminars. This led him to the belief our world is created by our thoughts words and actions. Taking this knowledge he then went on to create a tremendous amount of wealth over the next few decades. Something was missing as he found that money, good health, and success were not enough. This is Joe's story of how he found the missing piece.

www.ingramcontent.com/pod-product-compliance
Lightning Source LLC
Chambersburg PA
CBHW021402090426
42742CB00009B/966
9781599304113